TO SERVE WITHOUT FAVOR

Policing, Human Rights, and Accountability in Northern Ireland

Human Rights Watch/Helsinki

Human Rights Watch
New York · Washington · London · Brussels

ISBN 1-56432-216-5
Library of Congress Catalog Card Number: 97-73331

Cover photograph copyright © 1996 by Oistín Mac Bride. RUC riot squad in Drumcree.

Addresses for Human Rights Watch
485 Fifth Avenue, New York, NY 10017-6104
Tel: (212) 972-8400, Fax: (212) 972-0905, E-mail: hrwnyc@hrw.org

1522 K Street, N.W., #910, Washington, DC 20005-1202
Tel: (202) 371-6592, Fax: (202) 371-0124, E-mail: hrwdc@hrw.org

33 Islington High Street, N1 9LH London, UK
Tel: (171) 713-1995, Fax: (171) 713-1800, E-mail: hrwatchuk@gn.apc.org

15 Rue Van Campenhout, 1000 Brussels, Belgium
Tel: (2) 732-2009, Fax: (2) 732-0471, E-mail: hrwatchcu@gn.apc.org

Web Site Address: http://www.hrw.org
Gopher Address://gopher.humanrights.org:5000/11/int/Human Rights Watch
Listserv address: To subscribe to the list, send an e-mail message to majordomo@igc.apc.org with "subscribe Human Rights Watch-news" in the body of the message (leave the subject line blank).

HUMAN RIGHTS WATCH

Human Rights Watch conducts regular, systematic investigations of human rights abuses in some seventy countries around the world. Our reputation for timely, reliable disclosures has made us an essential source of information for those concerned with human rights. We address the human rights practices of governments of all political stripes, of all geopolitical alignments, and of all ethnic and religious persuasions. Human Rights Watch defends freedom of thought and expression, due process and equal protection of the law, and a vigorous civil society; we document and denounce murders, disappearances, torture, arbitrary imprisonment, discrimination, and other abuses of internationally recognized human rights. Our goal is to hold governments accountable if they transgress the rights of their people.

Human Rights Watch began in 1978 with the founding of its Helsinki division. Today, it includes five divisions covering Africa, the Americas, Asia, the Middle East, as well as the signatories of the Helsinki accords. It also includes three collaborative projects on arms transfers, children's rights, and women's rights. It maintains offices in New York, Washington, Los Angeles, London, Brussels, Moscow, Dushanbe, Rio de Janeiro, and Hong Kong. Human Rights Watch is an independent, nongovernmental organization, supported by contributions from private individuals and foundations worldwide. It accepts no government funds, directly or indirectly.

The staff includes Kenneth Roth, executive director; Michele Alexander, development director; Cynthia Brown, program director; Barbara Guglielmo, finance and administration director; Robert Kimzey, publications director; Jeri Laber, special advisor; Lotte Leicht, Brussels office director; Susan Osnos, communications director; Jemera Rone, counsel; Wilder Tayler, general counsel; and Joanna Weschler, United Nations representative.

The regional directors of Human Rights Watch are Peter Takirambudde, Africa; José Miguel Vivanco, Americas; Sidney Jones, Asia; Holly Cartner, Helsinki; and Eric Goldstein, Middle East (acting). The project directors are Joost R. Hiltermann, Arms Project; Lois Whitman, Children's Rights Project; and Dorothy Q. Thomas, Women's Rights Project.

The members of the board of directors are Robert L. Bernstein, chair; Adrian W. DeWind, vice chair; Roland Algrant, Lisa Anderson, William Carmichael, Dorothy Cullman, Gina Despres, Irene Diamond, Fiona Druckenmiller, Edith Everett, Jonathan Fanton, James C. Goodale, Jack Greenberg, Vartan Gregorian, Alice H. Henkin, Stephen L. Kass, Marina Pinto Kaufman, Bruce Klatsky, Harold Hongju Koh, Alexander MacGregor, Josh Mailman, Samuel K. Murumba, Andrew Nathan, Jane Olson, Peter Osnos, Kathleen Peratis, Bruce Rabb, Sigrid Rausing, Anita Roddick, Orville Schell, Sid Sheinberg, Gary G. Sick, Malcolm Smith, Domna Stanton, Maureen White, and Maya Wiley.

ACKNOWLEDGMENTS

This report is based on a mission conducted by Julia A. Hall, W. Bradford Wiley Fellow with Human Rights Watch, Hon. Robert M. Levy, United States Magistrate Judge in the Eastern District of New York, and Jonathan F. Fanton, president of the New School for Social Reseach, in November 1996. The report was written by Ms. Hall and edited by Holly Cartner, executive director of Human Rights Watch/Helsinki, Michael McClintock, deputy program director of Human Rights Watch, and Dinah PoKempner, deputy counsel with Human Rights Watch. Emily Shaw provided production assistance.

Human Rights Watch is grateful for the assistance of a number of colleagues in the preparation of the mission and the completion of this report, particularly Martin Flaherty, associate professor at Fordham University School of Law and consultant to the Lawyers Committee for Human Rights; Ann Gaughan, American Protestants for Truth about Ireland; and Halya Gowan, Amnesty International. We are especially indebted to Jane Winter of British-Irish Rights Watch in London, and Martin O'Brien, Paul Mageean, and Maggie Beirne of the Committee on the Administration of Justice in Belfast. Without their expertise and generosity, this mission would not have been possible. The writer also wishes to thank Chief Constable Ronnie Flanagan of the Royal Ulster Constabulary for his willingness to grant Human Rights Watch unprecedented access to RUC management, and for the careful attention paid by RUC staff in the chief constable's office to numerous requests for additional information in the months following the mission.

CONTENTS

ABBREVIATIONS AND ACRONYMS

AI	Amnesty International
BIRW	British Irish Rights Watch
BRG	Bogside Residents Group
CAJ	Committee on the Administration of Justice
CLMC	Combined Loyalist Military Command
DAAD	Direct Action Against Drugs
DOE	Department of Environment
DPP	Director of Public Prosecutions
DRPA	Dunloy Residents and Parents Association
DUP	Democratic Unionist Party
ECHR	European Convention on Human Rights
EPA	Northern Ireland (Emergency Provisions) Act 1996
FAIT	Families Against Intimidation and Terror
GRRC	Garvaghy Road Residents Coalition
HMIC	Her Majesty's Inspectorate of Constabulary
ICCPR	International Covenant on Civil and Political Rights
ICHC	Independent Commissioner for the Holding Centres
ICPC	Independent Commission for Police Complaints
IRA	Irish Republican Army
LOCC	Lower Ormeau Concerned Community
MI5	British military intelligence
MP	Member of Parliament
NIO	Northern Ireland Office
PACE	Police and Criminal Evidence (Northern Ireland) Order 1989
PANI	Police Authority for Northern Ireland
PTA	Prevention of Terrorism (Temporary Provisions) Act 1989
PUP	Progressive Unionist Party
RUC	Royal Ulster Constabulary
SACHR	Standing Advisory Commission on Human Rights
SAS	British Army Special Air Services Regiment
SDLP	Social Democratic and Labour Party
STAC	Stop Think and Change Program
UDA	Ulster Defense Association
UDP	Ulster Democratic Party
UDR	Ulster Defense Regiment
UFF	Ulster Freedom Fighters
UUP	Ulster Unionist Party
UVF	Ulster Volunteer Force

I swear by Almighty God that I will well and truly serve our Sovereign Lady the Queen in the office of constable without favour or affection, malice or ill-will; that I will to the best of my power cause the peace to be kept and preserved and that I will prevent to the best of my power all offences against the same; and that, while I shall continue to hold the said office, I will faithfully, according to the law, to the best of my skill and knowledge, discharge all the duties of the said office and all such duties as may be attached to such office by law and that I do not now belong to and that I will not, while I shall hold the said office, belong to any association, society, or confederacy formed for or engaged in any seditious purpose, or any purpose tending to disturb the public peace, or in any way disloyal to our Sovereign Lady the Queen and that I will not, while I shall hold the said office, engage or take part in the furthering of any such purpose, or take or administer, or assist or be present at or consent to the administering of, any oath or engagement binding myself or any other person to engage in any such purpose.

- *The Oath of Office sworn by constables in Northern Ireland*

1. INTRODUCTION

This report is about policing, human rights and accountability in Northern Ireland. Police conduct throughout the long conflict in Northern Ireland has given rise to serious allegations of abuse. A range of such allegations, examined in this report, continue to center on the Royal Ulster Constabulary (RUC), Northern Ireland's police force. The report also examines abuses by the political armed groups operating in Northern Ireland—republican paramilitaries seeking to reunite Northern Ireland with the Republic of Ireland and loyalist paramilitaries seeking to maintain the union of Northern Ireland with the United Kingdom. This report is, in part, an extension of past work by Human Rights Watch on the human rights situation in Northern Ireland and on the treatment of children there.

The report is also a direct response to the final report of the International Body on Arms Decommissioning chaired by former United States Senator George Mitchell. In late 1995, the British and Irish governments tasked an independent international body with providing to the multi-party peace talks an acceptable plan for the full and verifiable decommissioning of paramilitary weapons. Released in January 1996, the report of the International Body on Arms Decommissioning was welcomed in many quarters as a blueprint for progress from preparatory talks to full peace negotiations. Notably, the International Body recognized that success in the peace process could not be achieved solely by focusing on the decommissioning of weapons. To create the necessary trust, it concluded, confidence-building measures would also be necessary, including the normalization of policing, a review of the use of plastic bullets, a more balanced representation on the police force, and the cessation of paramilitary intimidation. All of these issues are addressed in this report.

The recent course of events in Northern Ireland has forced the issue of police reform to the forefront of public discourse. On August 31, 1994, the Irish Republican Army (IRA) announced a unilateral cease-fire. On October 13, 1994, the Combined Loyalist Paramilitary Command (CLMC), the coordinating body representing loyalist paramilitary groups, followed suit and called for a cessation of "all operational hostilities." Questions arose immediately about the need for security policing and the continuation of emergency laws in the absence of political violence. Calls went out for the redress of the profound religious imbalance in the composition of the RUC, which is approximately 90 percent Protestant. Discussions in many quarters during the cease-fire period focused on police accountability and the need for reform of a "security dependent" system that appeared to leave the RUC accountable to virtually no one.

Although the report of the International Body recommended that the process for paramilitary arms decommissioning run parallel to the peace talks and opined that a total surrender of weapons prior to negotiations was not reasonable, the British government refused to allow Sinn Féin, which is generally viewed as the political arm of the IRA, to participate in the talks until the IRA decommissioned its weapons. In January 1996 the Northern Ireland (Emergency Provisions) Act (EPA) was renewed for another two years even though the cease-fires had held since late 1994. The Prevention of Terrorism (Temporary Provisions) Act (PTA) covering all of the U.K. was also renewed during the cease-fire period. Disagreements over decommissioning, the role of the Irish government in the preparatory talks, and the condition of Irish prisoners in British prisons plagued the multi-party talks. By late January 1996, there appeared to be a loss of confidence in the peace process.

On February 9, 1996, the IRA broke its cease-fire with the explosion of a bomb at Canary Wharf in London, killing two men and injuring more than 100 people. The IRA cease-fire was broken in Northern Ireland in October 1996 with a bombing at British army barracks at Lisburn, County Antrim. One soldier was killed and dozens of people were injured. In a New Year's statement published in *An Phoblacht/Republican News*, the IRA reaffirmed its "steadfast commitment" to reunifying Northern Ireland with the Republic of Ireland. This statement was widely perceived as the IRA's confirmation of the resumption of full-scale military operations in pursuit of this goal.

From December 1996 to April 1997, the IRA claimed responsibility for a number of attacks on RUC stations and police officers. One part-time policewoman was shot and seriously injured. A British soldier was shot and killed by an IRA sniper. As of May 15, 1997, the CLMC claimed that the loyalist paramilitary cease-fire was holding despite a number of bombings and shootings bearing the hallmark of loyalist paramilitary violence. Since December 1996, there has been an intensification in security measures causing many to compare the atmosphere in Northern Ireland to the tension-filled and violent years immediately preceding the cease-fires.

This report focuses on four areas of policing that are of immediate human rights concern: the draconian police powers enjoyed by the RUC under Northern Ireland's emergency regime, the policing of the summer 1996 marching season (when Protestant fraternal orders paraded through towns and city centers), the dramatic rise in paramilitary punishment assaults and expulsions, and the persistent allegations of collusion between members of the security forces and loyalist paramilitary groups.

The British government has responded to the conflict in Northern Ireland by imposing a draconian emergency regime that invests the RUC with expansive police powers to stop, question, search, arrest, detain, and interrogate persons merely suspected of terrorist activity. For example, people can be stopped, questioned and searched without "reasonable suspicion" of criminal activity; detainees can be held for up to seven days without charge; access to counsel can be deferred for the first forty-eight hours of detention; and the common law right to silence has been effectively abrogated. In holding centers, specially designated places of detention for persons arrested under the emergency legislation, the intimidation and harassment of detainees and lawyers representing them is commonplace. Interrogations are not audio or video taped, and the EPA contains a permissive standard for the admissibility of confession evidence at trial.

In 1991, Human Rights Watch reported that the operation of the emergency legislation in Northern Ireland gave rise to systematic human rights violations and argued for the repeal of emergency laws that unduly infringed civil liberties and were used for harassment and intimidation. We renew that call for repeal in this report. Particularly with the planned resumption of multi-party talks in June 1997, we urge the government of the United Kingdom to recognize that emergency laws such as those in force in Northern Ireland often serve to sustain political violence by creating an environment in which individual human rights are routinely violated. Further inaction on the repeal of the emergency laws will sustain the historic climate of distrust and hostility between the government of the United Kingdom and certain segments of its citizenry. This is hardly a promising context within which to advance the peace.

While the emergency legislation provides the backdrop for routinely abusive police practices, the outbreak of serious violence during the summer 1996 marching season demonstrated how policing failures and the lack of accountability for RUC misconduct contributed to a serious breakdown in the rule of law. The apparent context for the disturbances of the summer of 1996 was the ongoing dispute between Protestant fraternal orders and predominantly Catholic nationalist communities that had organized to oppose Protestant marches through Catholic areas. The fraternal orders portray their processions as traditional marches that give expression to their religious and cultural heritage, and argue that their right to free assembly is unduly infringed by nationalist opposition. Nationalist groups characterize the marches as sectarian parades that often incite hatred by providing the traditionally privileged unionists—Protestants in favor of maintaining the union of Northern Ireland with the United Kingdom—with a forum in which to re-enact historic triumphs of Protestants over Catholics. Nationalists also argue that the heavy police presence accompanying the marches, which is often characterized by intimidating operational tactics, disproportionately disrupts the life of nationalist communities.

However, to cast the summer's events simply as a matter of intercommunal conflict fails to address the responsibility of state authorities in Northern Ireland to maintain the rule of law and to assure both communities the equal protection of their rights. This includes the grievous failure of the police, oversight agencies, and the British government to prevent the collapse of law and order. Despite RUC claims of being caught in the middle of disputes between nationalists and unionists over the "right to march," a series of police actions—sanctioned by the government—exacerbated the conflict. These actions resulted in the effective submission of state authorities to the threat of unionist violence and included the excessive use of force against peaceful demonstrators, the indiscriminate use of plastic bullets against both unionist and nationalist protesters, and a general failure to halt illegal activities such as the blockade of the airport and the establishment of illegal roadblocks.

The serious violence that erupted during the summer of 1996 demonstrated the volatile circumstances in which the people of Northern Ireland negotiate the annual, tension-filled marching season. In addition, both nationalist and unionist communities must daily confront the brutal violence of paramilitary punishment beatings and assaults. Both republican and loyalist paramilitary organizations have assumed a quasi-policing role in their respective communities by meting out "punishments" for perceived or actual offenses, such as drug trafficking, burglary, assault, wife abuse, glue sniffing, public intoxication, joyriding and other "anti-social" activities. These non-political offenses, which would be addressed through routine policing by a traditional police force, have instead been effectively delegated to irregular, paramilitary "law enforcement." Paramilitary punishments take a variety of forms, including summary executions (murders), crippling shootings, and brutal beatings. They are carried out by paramilitary volunteers against members of their own communities. Paramilitary organizations also issue "expulsion orders" to force an alleged perpetrator to leave a particular city or all of Northern Ireland for a designated period under threat of being shot or beaten.

The IRA and loyalist paramilitary groups such as the Ulster Defense Association (UDA) and the Ulster Volunteer Force (UVF) operate parallel unofficial criminal justice systems in the vacuum left by the police. Throughout "the troubles" in Northern Ireland, the police have concentrated their efforts on the suppression of political violence by paramilitary groups. This anti-terrorist campaign has been waged to the exclusion of many traditional policing functions in some areas. For example, in many nationalist communities, routine foot patrols were rare and RUC land rover patrols were often backed up by British military vehicles. Both nationalists and unionists allege that in some areas the RUC does not respond to calls requesting assistance with ordinary crimes or, if the police do respond, officers often pick up "suspects" only in an attempt to persuade them to serve as political informers while ignoring the reported crime. The expansive police powers enjoyed by the RUC under Northern Ireland's emergency legislation further contributes to the notion that the RUC is not a traditional police force and it need not bother with such quotidian duties as responding to common crime. Research undertaken by Human Rights Watch confirmed that in many communities in Northern Ireland normal policing functions have been abandoned. Moreover, in the post-cease-fire period, many of the policing initiatives cited by the RUC as attempts to "normalize" policing have been sacrificed to intensified anti-terrorism security measures.

In the absence of normal policing, paramilitary organizations act as investigator, prosecutor, judge and jury, and they carry out their own sentences. Warnings are sometimes given before shootings or beatings but even crude due process guarantees are generally dispensed with in favor of summary proceedings. The paramilitaries euphemistically label "community policing" what in fact are brutal punishments applied in an often arbitrary manner.

The final issue addressed in this report is the persistent allegations of collusion between members of the security forces in Northern Ireland and loyalist paramilitary groups. Security forces allegedly engage in such collusion by conspiring directly with loyalist paramilitaries to carry out acts of violence or by facilitating the commission of violent loyalist paramilitary activities. The failure to prevent or deter violent acts for which there is reliable advance intelligence or to investigate rigorously such acts and punish those responsible can also constitute collusion. Those who allege collusion charge that members of the security forces routinely engage in a variety of illegal activities to assist loyalist paramilitary groups to target suspected republican "terrorists" or alleged "terrorist" sympathizers for harassment and assassination. In addition to allegations of direct involvement in the planning and execution of assassinations, security forces have been accused of passing on security information such as photo montages to loyalist paramilitaries who use the information to target suspected republican "terrorists," facilitating the commission of loyalist paramilitary killings by diverting law enforcement resources away from crime scenes immediately prior to and after paramilitary shootings, failing to provide adequate protection to persons warned by the security forces that they are under paramilitary threat because their security files "accidentally" went missing or were "lost," and failing to investigate rigorously loyalist paramilitary killings by overlooking critical and easily accessible forensic evidence.

Human Rights Watch is particularly concerned with allegations of collusion against the police force in Northern Ireland. Because the RUC is invested with primary responsibility for identifying, gathering and securing information on suspected paramilitaries and investigating acts of paramilitary violence, the bulk of the allegations of collusion are made against the RUC. This is particularly true in cases where legitimately collected official information finds its way into the hands of loyalist paramilitaries.

Collusion, by definition, is difficult to prove. Human Rights Watch makes no conclusions regarding the evidence of collusion by the RUC in any of the cases highlighted in this report. However, the factors suggesting the possibility of collusion associated with these cases compel us to call for a variety of immediate official responses to determine whether collusion has occurred. In some cases an independent inquiry with full investigative powers, including the power to subpoena witnesses and documents, is recommended. In other cases, we call on the RUC to take specific steps to ensure that factors suggesting collusion are adequately addressed. General recommendations for the effective redress of possible collusion include: a reassessment of the procedures for the handling of identification information for security breaches; vetting the police force for members with illicit associations to loyalist paramilitary groups; commitment to rigorous investigations of paramilitary killings in conformity with international standards; and a review of inquest procedures in Northern Ireland which at present appear designed to deny families access to information about possible security force involvement in the killing of a family member.

The recent change of government in the United Kingdom may open a new chapter in Northern Ireland's troubled history. Newly appointed Secretary of State Dr. Marjorie Mowlam has promised to join the people of Northern Ireland in confronting the obstacles that remain to achieving a new political settlement. To that end, the new government has promised a number of new initiatives to build confidence throughout Northern Ireland including the expansion and reinforcement of individual rights and the reform of policing. Labour's commitment to confidence-building measures, particularly its express reference to the promotion of human rights, is most welcome. Human Rights Watch seeks to capitalize on the moment by contributing directly to a fuller understanding of how the erosion of human rights and civil liberties has exacerbated the conflict in Northern Ireland.

2. RECOMMENDATIONS

Human Rights Watch makes the following recommendations to the government of the United Kingdom:

The Emergency Regime

- The emergency regime in Northern Ireland should be dismantled, beginning immediately, with the repeal of provisions of the Northern Ireland (Emergency Provisions Act) 1996 (EPA) and the Prevention of Terrorism (Temporary Provisions) Act 1989 (PTA) that unduly infringe civil liberties and are used by the police to harass and intimidate people.

- A "reasonable suspicion" of criminal activity should be required for the police to exercise the powers to stop, question and search people. The U.K. government should take immediate steps to end random street stops and searches and to ensure that all searches are conducted without degrading or harassing measures.

- The EPA's search and entry powers should be repealed. A judicial warrant should be required for house searches and for examining or seizing documents.

- The U.K. government should withdraw its derogation to article 5(3) of the European Convention on Human Rights which allows the police to detain persons arrested under the emergency legislation for up to seven days without charge.

- Detainees should be brought before a court within at least forty-eight hours of arrest.

- Castlereagh Holding Centre should be closed immediately in compliance with the recommendations of the U.N. Human Rights Committee and the U.N. Committee Against Torture. These U.N. bodies and the U.K.-appointed Independent Commissioner for the Holding Centres have found the conditions of detention in Castlereagh "unacceptable" due to tiny cells with no natural light, the absence of exercise areas, lengthy and frequent interrogations, and persistent allegations of intimidation and harassment during interrogations.

•   The U.K. should immediately take the following steps to comply with the 1996 decision of the European Court of Human Rights in *Murray v. United Kingdom* which held that the abrogation of the right to silence in combination with restrictions on access to counsel amount to a violation of the fair trial provisions of the European Convention for the Protection of Human Rights and Fundamental Freedoms (ECHR):

> 1) The Criminal Evidence (Northern Ireland) Order 1988, which permits a court to draw adverse inferences from a suspect's refusal to answer questions asked by police during interrogations and at trial, should be rescinded as an unjustified infringement of the privilege against self-incrimination.
>
> 2) Detainees should have prompt and regular access to counsel of their choice and detainees should be allowed to have their lawyers present during interrogations.

•   The Independent Commissioner for the Holding Centres' (ICHC) proposal for the establishment of a legal advice unit at holding centers, which would modify the present legal aid system in Northern Ireland by granting legal aid only to those detainees arrested under the emergency legislation who choose a government-appointed solicitor from a unit of lawyers associated with the holding centers, should be rejected. Detainees should have prompt access to a lawyer of their choice.

•   Detainees should be able to notify family members or friends immediately following arrest.

•   The RUC should take immediate effective measures to prevent the physical and psychological ill-treatment of detainees. Officers who carry out such abuses should be disciplined and criminally prosecuted.

•   All interrogations should be audio and video taped. Detainees' attorneys should have access to all audio and video tapes of interrogations.

•   The permissive EPA standard for admitting at trial confession evidence procured by psychological pressure, deprivation, or other non-violent forms of coercion should be abolished. The standard for admitting confession evidence should conform to the ordinary criminal law, the Police and Criminal Evidence (Northern Ireland) Order 1989 (PACE), which excludes confession evidence that was obtained by oppression or "in consequence of anything said or done which was likely, in the circumstances existing at the time, to render unreliable any confession which might be made. . . in consequence thereof."

• The juryless Diplock courts, established to try political violence cases, have caused a loss of confidence in the justice system and should be abolished. The common law right to trial by jury should be restored in Northern Ireland involving, if necessary, measures to protect jurors.

Police Accountability
• The current tripartite structure responsible for policing in Northern Ireland—involving the inter-relationship of the U.K. government, the RUC, and the civilian oversight Police Authority for Northern Ireland—should be reformed to provide for greater public accountability for the RUC. The Police Authority, in practice excluded from participation in the determination of policies related to security policing and the operational aspects of policing in Northern Ireland, should be consulted on security and operational matters and its recommendations taken into consideration.

• The U.K. government should establish an independent unit to investigate complaints against police officers as recommended by Dr. Maurice Hayes, independent reviewer of the police-complaints system appointed by the U.K. government.

• All RUC officers should be required to take instruction in basic human rights guarantees which the force is obliged to respect in compliance with the U.K.'s international obligations, including the International Covenant on Civil and Political Rights (ICCPR), the European Convention for the Protection of Human Rights and Fundamental Freedoms (ECHR), the Convention Against Torture (CAT), the Convention on the Elimination of Racial Discrimination (CERD), and international codes of conduct for law enforcement officials and the use of firearms.

Composition of the RUC

• Progressive measures should commence immediately to rectify the religious imbalance in the RUC. RUC management should develop a strategy for attracting and securing positions on the force for qualified Catholic applicants. The Police Authority for Northern Ireland should be consulted in this process and its recommendations taken into consideration.

Policing Parades and Marches

• An independent body should make determinations concerning conditions on marches and parades.

• Decisions taken by the secretary of state for Northern Ireland to ban marches should be judicially reviewable.

• The police should take measures to ensure that the right to peaceful assembly is protected to the greatest possible extent. Assemblies that pose a threat of violence should be restricted only to the extent necessary in a democratic society in the interest of public safety.

• The police should take measures to ensure that the rights to freedom of movement and privacy in the communities through which marches pass are protected. If restrictions on movement are required, they should be proportionate to the interest advanced by state authorities.

• The use of plastic bullets should be banned because they have killed fourteen people in Northern Ireland, including seven children, and severely injured hundreds of others. Alternative methods of crowd control should be developed and employed.

• Lethal force should be used in Northern Ireland only when necessary to meet an imminent threat to life and only in proportion to the actual danger presented in conformity with international standards.

• Police should be adequately trained to defuse tense situations non-violently.

• Policing of marches and parades should be conducted impartially and professionally. Officers should not use sectarian language in the course of any police operation. Disciplinary measures should be taken against those who violate these principles.

• The death of Dermot McShane, who was killed after a British army armored personnel carrier ran over him under suspicious circumstances during the summer of 1996 disturbances, should be investigated in conformity with the United Nations Principles on the Effective Prevention and Investigation of Extra-Legal, Arbitrary and Summary Executions.

Punishment Shootings, Assaults, and Expulsions

• The IRA and loyalist paramilitary organizations should immediately halt punishment shootings, beatings, and expulsions.

• The RUC should perform normal policing functions in all areas of Northern Ireland. The U.K. government should provide adequate training, resources and protection for police officers carrying out such duties.

• Political parties in Northern Ireland should not support the creation of alternative "justice" systems in communities.

Allegations of Collusion

• The police force should be vetted thoroughly to identify and exclude recruits, officers, and reservists with illicit connections to paramilitary groups.

• Procedures for the handling of security information should be reassessed with a view to eliminating security breaches such as the leaking of photo montages.

• Measures should be taken by the U.K. government to afford persons under threat from paramilitary organizations the greatest possible protection, including the approval of home security grants.

• In areas where paramilitary killings have occurred or killings have been threatened, security measures should be implemented on routes into and out of those communities to ensure that they receive adequate protection from incursions by paramilitaries.

- The RUC should rigorously investigate paramilitary killings, including by using good forensic practices.

- Allegations that detectives conducting interrogations threaten to pass a detainee's security information to paramilitary organizations should be investigated rigorously. Officers found guilty of such an abuse should be punished.

- Special efforts should be made to protect lawyers who represent suspects charged under the emergency legislation from interference, harassment, intimidation, or death threats from RUC detectives. Allegations of intimidation of defense lawyers should be investigated, and offending officers should be punished.

- An independent, public inquiry into the killing of Catholic criminal defense lawyer Patrick Finucane, with powers to administer oaths and to subpoena witnesses, should be convened.

- The U.K. government should permit the discovery of information relevant to the murder of Patrick Finucane for use in Geraldine Finucane's civil action and application to the European Court of Human Rights (ECHR).

- The RUC should investigate the murder of Patrick Shanaghan, who suffered years of official harassment and threats before being killed by loyalist paramilitaries, in compliance with the United Nations Principles on the Effective Prevention and Investigation of Extra-Legal, Arbitrary and Summary Executions.

- The complaints of Patrick Shanaghan's mother, Mary Shanaghan, to the Independent Commission for Police Complaints (ICPC) should be investigated rigorously and appropriate action should be taken against any officers found to have acted in violation of RUC policy or of British law.

- The Coroners' Law and Rules for Northern Ireland should, at a minimum, be brought in line with the law and rules for England and Wales; for example, coroner's juries should have the power to reach a full verdict, such as "unlawful killing by unnamed person(s)."

- Persons suspected of causing the death at issue should be compelled to testify in person, but should not be required to answer questions that might incriminate them.

- Families of victims and their attorneys should have access to all the evidence to be introduced at an inquest and adequate time to prepare for their interventions.

3. POLICING NORTHERN IRELAND

The British government seems to have refused to learn the obvious lesson which the past twenty years should have taught it so clearly: if emergency powers which are open to abuse are created, the pressure of the emergency is such that these powers will be abused.[1]

Introduction

Policing in Northern Ireland must be set within the context of the extraordinary measures taken by the United Kingdom to address the civil unrest and paramilitary violence that have characterized "the Troubles." The security policies pursued by the U.K. have resulted in the imposition of draconian emergency legislation which invests the Royal Ulster Constabulary (RUC), the Northern Ireland police force, with expansive police powers to stop, question, search, arrest, detain, and interrogate persons suspected of "terrorist" activity. The emergency regime co-exists with criminal laws that govern so-called "normal" criminal activities, that is, crimes of a non-political nature such as ordinary burglary or domestic violence. This dual criminal justice system creates a category of offender—the "suspected terrorist"—whose human rights are subordinate to the pursuit of the state's security policies.

It is undisputed that individual human rights suffer in situations of public emergency.[2] In 1991, Helsinki Watch reported that the operation of the emergency legislation in Northern Ireland had given rise to systematic human rights violations and we argued for the repeal of emergency laws which unduly infringed civil liberties and were used to harass and intimidate people.[3]

---

[1]Kevin Boyle and Colm Campbell, *Human Rights in Situations of Armed Conflict and Political Violence* (Santiago Chile: SINERGOS Consultores, Ltda., 1992), p. 20.

[2]See Ninth Annual Report of the United Nations Special Rapporteur on Human Rights and States of Emergency, *The Administration of Justice and the Human Rights of Detainees: Question of Human Rights and States of Emergency*, E/CN.4/Sub.2/1996/19, June 18, 1996.

[3]Helsinki Watch, *Human Rights in Northern Ireland* (New York: Human Rights Watch, 1991), p. 143. Helsinki Watch has since been renamed Human Rights Watch/Helsinki.

14

The paramilitary cease-fires[4] gave human rights groups renewed impetus to advocate for the repeal of emergency legislation based on the near absence of political violence in Northern Ireland.[5] To the dismay of many local groups and international bodies, the government did not use the cease-fire period to evaluate genuinely the need for emergency laws.[6] Indeed, the cease-fire period saw not only the renewal of emergency legislation in January 1996 but a strengthening of some provisions in these laws. The Labour Party, a traditional opponent of renewal, abstained in the 1996 vote leaving the Prevention of Terrorism Act (PTA) renewal to pass with virtually no debate. The failure of the government to build confidence in the rule of law and the administration of justice by initiating a process for dismantling the emergency regime had a profoundly negative effect on confidence in the peace process.

This background chapter is not a comprehensive evaluation of the operation of the emergency legislation at this time. It reviews the emergency police powers currently in use by the RUC and notes recent jurisprudential and procedural developments with respect to these powers. Structures for police accountability in Northern Ireland and the composition of the RUC are also discussed.

---

[4]The Irish Republican Army (IRA) cease-fire commenced on August 31, 1994, and ended on February 9, 1996. The Combined Loyalist Military Command (CLMC) cease-fire commenced on October 13, 1994. The CLMC cease-fire holds despite a number of violent incidents which have put its status in doubt. The cease-fire period discussed herein is the period during which both the IRA and loyalist paramilitaries ceased all political violence. (See Introduction to this report.)

[5]Committee on the Administration of Justice, *No Emergency, No Emergency Law: Emergency Legislation Related to Northern Ireland, The Case for Repeal* (Belfast: CAJ, March 1995). The European Court of Human Rights requires a level of violence which poses a "threat to the life of the nation" to justify the imposition of emergency measures which derogate from the convention's provisions. In 1989, the U.K. derogated from the ECHR citing security concerns. The derogation was not withdrawn during the cease-fires. (See section below on "Extended Police Custody.")

[6]See U.N. Human Rights Committee, *Comments of the Human Rights Committee in Consideration of the Fourth Periodic Report of the United Kingdom and Northern Ireland*, CCPR/C/79/Add.55, July 27, 1995, para. 11; U.N. Committee Against Torture, *Consideration of Second Periodic Report of the United Kingdom of Great Britain and Northern Ireland and Dependent Territories*, CAT/C/SR.234/Add.1, paras. 26, 53, 67, 79.

The Emergency Regime in Northern Ireland

Emergency powers provide the backdrop for many of the events described in this report. There has been an intensification of security measures under the emergency legislation in Northern Ireland since the IRA bombing of British army headquarters at Thiepval barracks in Lisburn in October 1996 and the escalation of paramilitary violence beginning in December 1996. It is regrettable that, with the exception of a reduction in widespread physical abuse in detention centers, most of the conclusions and recommendations from our 1991 report with respect to the emergency legislation remain relevant. With the resumption of multi-party talks in June 1997, we urge the government of the United Kingdom to recognize that emergency laws such as those in force in Northern Ireland often serve to perpetuate political violence by creating an environment in which individual human rights are routinely violated. Further inaction on the repeal of the emergency laws will sustain the historic climate of distrust and hostility between the government of the United Kingdom and certain segments of its citizenry. This is hardly a promising context within which to advance the peace.

Emergency legislation has been in force in Northern Ireland since the partition of the island of Ireland in 1922. The emergency regime consists of a set of laws which, taken in combination, give the RUC extraordinary police powers. The Northern Ireland (Emergency Provisions) Act 1996 (EPA) applies only in Northern Ireland. This law, the latest in a series of amended versions to a 1973 act, replaced the Civil Authorities (Special Powers) Act (Northern Ireland)1922. The EPA was renewed in January 1996 for two years commencing in August 1996. The Prevention of Terrorism (Temporary Provisions) Act 1989 (PTA), first passed in 1974, applies across the United Kingdom, is renewable annually, and was extended for another year in March 1997.

In addition to specific pieces of anti-terrorism legislation, the emergency regime is fortified by regressive developments in the ordinary criminal law. Of particular concern is the Criminal Evidence (Northern Ireland) Order 1988 which effectively abrogates the common law right to silence.

The EPA and PTA are subject to periodic government-sponsored reviews which the government claims as measures of accountability for the oversight of the emergency regime. In October 1996, Lord Lloyd of Berwick issued a two volume *Inquiry into Legislation Against Terrorism*. The government's terms of reference for the inquiry instructed Lord Lloyd to "consider the future need for specific counter-terrorism legislation in the United Kingdom if the cessation of terrorism connected with the affairs of Northern Ireland leads to a lasting peace."[7] Although Lord Lloyd's recommendations included a number of positive steps toward dismantling the emergency regime as it existed during the course of his inquiry, with the resumption of IRA violence in February 1996, the government made no effort to implement any of the recommendations. Lord Lloyd himself stated that his recommendations "seem somewhat inapposite" in light of the end of the IRA cease-fire.[8] Unfortunately, Lord Lloyd's inquiry made the same presumption as past government-sponsored reviews—that emergency laws are necessary *until* peace is achieved. Human Rights Watch/Helsinki believes that the dismantling of the emergency regime now can contribute directly to achieving that peace.

Police Powers Under the Emergency Regime

Special powers enjoyed by the RUC under the emergency regime in Northern Ireland include:[9]

- **Stop, Question and Search:** Under section 25 of the EPA, the police may stop any person or vehicle "for so long as is necessary" to ascertain "that person's identity and movements" and what a person may know "concerning any recent explosion or any other recent incident endangering life or concerning any person killed or injured in any such explosion or incident." There is no requirement of reasonable suspicion. Under section 20(6)(a), an officer may search a person who has been stopped to determine if the person is carrying a weapon or transmitter.

- **House Searches:** Section 20 of the EPA allows the police to enter and search residences without a judicial warrant if they have reasonable grounds to believe that explosives, weapons or other terrorist contraband is present. Occupants of a house being searched may be required to stay in one part of the house for up to four hours with an extension of another four hours upon the recommendation of a police officer of the rank of

---

[7]Rt. Hon. Lord Lloyd of Berwick, *Inquiry into Legislation Against Terrorism* (London: HMSO, October 1996), p. v.

[8]Ibid., p. I.

[9]Information for this section borrows heavily from Helsinki Watch, *Human Rights in Northern Ireland*, pp. 11-43; and Committee on the Administration of Justice, *No Emergency, No Emergency Law*, Chapters 4-7.

superintendent or above. This practice can amount to a form of house arrest.

- **Arrest Powers:** The arrest powers under the EPA are rarely used because the police enjoy broader authority to arrest and wider investigatory powers under the PTA. PTA section 14 permits a police officer to arrest without a warrant a person whom she or he has reasonable grounds to suspect of being guilty of an offense under certain provisions of the PTA which prohibit membership in or support of proscribed organizations or who is or has been concerned in the commission, preparation or instigation of acts of terrorism.

These powers allow the police to stop, question, and search people without any suspicion of criminal activity. Moreover, given the vague definition of terrorism ("the use of violence for political ends, including any use of violence for the purpose of putting the public or any section of the public in fear"), police have the authority to arrest on the most limited suspicion, information or intelligence.

The RUC is invested with special powers to detain and interrogate "suspects" under the emergency regime. These powers have been subject to criticism by various human rights bodies and in some important cases have been found to be in violation of the European Convention for the Protection of Human Rights and Fundamental Freedoms (ECHR). The right to silence, a cornerstone of the English common law, has been seriously eroded by developments in the ordinary criminal law in the United Kingdom. Moreover, persons charged under the EPA or PTA are tried in Diplock courts by a single judge sitting without a jury.[10] The civil liberties and human rights of people in Northern Ireland have been compromised severely in the following areas under the emergency regime:

- **Extended Police Custody:** Section 14 of the PTA permits a person who has been arrested to be detained for up to forty-eight hours. This initial detention period can be extended for up to five days upon authorization

---

[10]The Diplock courts are named after Lord Diplock whose recommendations concerning effective anti-terrorism measures, issued in 1972, are the basis of the EPA. The Diplock Commission reported that jury trials were "not practicable in the case of terrorist crimes in Northern Ireland due to 1) the threat of intimidation of witnesses and jurors; and 2) the possibility of "perverse verdicts," meaning verdicts based on political or sectarian grounds, rather than on evidence adduced during the trial of a case. Helsinki Watch, *Human Rights in Northern Ireland*, p. 86.

by the secretary of state. Thus, a detainee can be held for up to seven days without charge. In a 1988 case, the European Court of Human Rights held that a detention under the PTA for four days and six hours violated the fair trial provisions of article 5(3) of the ECHR.[11] In response, the United Kingdom entered a derogation under article 4 of the International Covenant on Civil and Political Rights (ICCPR) and article 15 of the ECHR in order to retain the seven day detention power. These articles permit a state signatory to suspend certain treaty obligations during an emergency which poses a "threat to the life of the nation."

- **Access to Counsel:** Section 47 of the EPA provides a detainee with the right to counsel if arrested under emergency provisions. However, access may be delayed for the first forty-eight hours of detention upon authorization by a senior police officer. Lawyers have not been permitted by the RUC to be present during interrogations.[12] In January 1996, a detainee, Christopher Hanley, sought judicial review of this policy. Before the case was heard, the RUC changed its policy stating that every request for counsel to be present during interrogations would be considered on the particular merits of each application. Hanley's request was reviewed anew and denied.[13] It has been reported that the RUC routinely denies applications for lawyer access to interrogations.[14]

---

[11]*Brogan, et. al., v. United Kingdom*, Series A, No. 145-B, Strasbourg, November 29, 1988.

[12]In October 1996, the Belfast High Court, Lord Chief Justice Hutton presiding, rejected a petitioner's argument that he had a right to have counsel present during interrogations. See *In the Matter of Applications by Michael Russell and Others for Judicial Review,* HUTE2184. However, Mr. Justice Kerr stated that while no such right has been extended by parliament, "it has not [been] pronounced...that access is forbidden. In my opinion, each application for access to a solicitor during interview should be considered individually." See *In the Matter of Applications by Michael Russell and Others for Judicial Review,* KERE2222, p. 5.

[13]"RUC Ban on Solicitors at Terrorist (sic) Interviews Lifted," *Belfast Telegraph,* January 25, 1996.

[14]Human Rights Watch/Helsinki interview with Peter Madden, Madden & Finucane Solicitors, Belfast, November 8, 1996.

- **Notification of Arrest:** EPA section 46 provides that persons detained under the emergency laws have the right to have a friend or relative informed of his or her arrest. However, notification may be delayed for up to forty-eight hours upon the authorization of an RUC superintendent. Members of the U.N. Committee Against Torture have expressed concern that deferral of notification of arrest coupled with deferral of access to counsel in the first forty-eight hours amounts to detention "incommunicado, thereby creating conditions which might lead to abuses of authority by agents of the State."[15]

- **Right to Silence:** The Criminal Evidence (Northern Ireland) Order 1988 has severely eroded the common law right to silence by permitting a judge to draw adverse inferences from a detainee's silence when he or she refuses to account for his or her presence at a particular place or to explain certain forensic evidence. Adverse inferences can also be drawn when a defendant, having been called to give evidence at trial, refuses to do so, or when a defendant offers for the first time at trial an explanation which a judge determines should have been offered during interrogation. In 1996, the European Court of Human Rights held in *Murray v. United Kingdom* that the power to draw adverse inferences from silence, coupled with the deferral of access to counsel in Northern Ireland, violated fair trial provisions of article 6 of the European Convention.[16] The government of the United Kingdom currently is "considering" the implications of the decision.[17]

---

[15]U.N. Committee Against Torture, *Consideration of First Periodic Report of the United Kingdom and Northern Ireland,* CAT/C/SR.91, November 15, 1991. The CAT reiterated its concern about incommunicado interrogation in the United Kingdom's second periodic report. See U.N. Committee Against Torture, *Consideration of Second Periodic Report of the United Kingdom of Great Britain and Northern Ireland,* para. 29.

[16]*Murray v. United Kingdom,* Case 41/1994/488/570 (1996). The privilege against self-incrimination is protected under article 14(3)(g) of the ICCPR and article 6(1) of the ECHR.

[17]Human Rights Watch/Helsinki interview with Sarah Todd, Northern Ireland Office, Belfast, November 12, 1996.

The physical conditions under which detainees are held and interrogated under the emergency legislation further emphasize the potential for police abuse. Moreover, standards for the admissibility of confession evidence under the EPA afford police detectives an extraordinary measure of protection against allegations of abuse during interrogations:

- **Holding Centers:** Suspects are kept in "holding centers," detention facilities for questioning persons arrested under the emergency laws. Three holding centers are currently in use in Northern Ireland: Castlereagh in Belfast, Gough Barracks in Armagh, and Strand Road in London/Derry.[18] In 1995, the U.N. Human Rights Committee recommended the closing of Castlereagh as a "matter of urgency" due to "unacceptable" conditions of detention, including tiny cells with no opening to natural light, the absence of exercise areas, lengthy and frequent interrogations, and persistent allegations of intimidation and harassment during interrogations.[19] The U.N. Committee Against Torture also recently expressed concern that interrogations at Castlereagh may breach the U.N. Convention Against Torture.[20] Notably, the government-appointed Independent Commissioner for the Holding Centres (ICHC), has called for the immediate closure of Castlereagh stating: "Each day that passes, the Government is in breach of its obligations to comply with the minimum standards for prisoners."[21]

---

[18]Unionists refer to this city as Londonderry; nationalists call it Derry. In this report, we refer to the city as London/Derry.

[19]U.N. Human Rights Committee, *Comments of the Human Rights Committee in Consideration of the Fourth Periodic Report of the United Kingdom and Northern Ireland*, para. 22. These "unacceptable conditions" are well-documented by British Irish Rights Watch in *Conditions in Castlereagh: Physical and Psychological Ill-Treatment of Detainees* (London: BIRW, October 1995).

[20]U.N. Committee Against Torture, *Consideration of Second Periodic Report of the United Kingdom of Great Britain and Northern Ireland and Dependent Territories*, para. 27.

[21]*Fourth Annual (1996) Report of the Independent Commissioner for the Holding Centres (Police Offices)* (Belfast: ICHC, March 10, 1997), p. 6. The Independent Commissioner, Sir Louis Blom-Cooper, was appointed by the U.K. government in 1992 in the aftermath of a U.N. Committee Against Torture report which severely criticized the

- **Monitoring Interrogations:** Currently, interrogations at holding centers are monitored by a closed circuit television network supervised by RUC officers who are responsible for viewing a bank of screens simultaneously.[22] There is no recording of any sort.[23] The Independent Commissioner for the Holding Centres, the Standing Advisory Commission on Human Rights (SACHR),[24] and numerous human rights organizations have called for the audio and video recording of all interrogations.[25] In January 1996, the secretary of state introduced plans for the silent video recording of interrogations.[26] To date, silent video recording has not been implemented in any of the holding centers. Expressing concern about persistent allegations of verbal abuse, intimidation and harassment by RUC detectives during interrogation, the Independent Commissioner for the Holding Centres has stated that silent video recording is insufficient because "[w]ithout accompanying words,

---

conditions of detention in holding centers. His mandate is to ensure that suspects detained under the emergency legislation are "fairly treated." *Independent Commissioner for the Holding Centres: Terms of Reference*, ICHC Handout, p. 1. Although it is within the mandate of the ICHC and his deputy to observe interrogations, by their own calculations, they have observed "something less than one-half of one percent" of all interviews conducted since 1992. *Fourth Annual (1996) Report*, p. 20.

[22]Human Rights Watch/Helsinki interview with Dr. William Norris, Deputy Independent Commissioner for the Holding Centres, Belfast, November 8, 1996.

[23]The RUC has argued against taping claiming that suspects might be less willing to volunteer "off the record" information—that is, to inform—in the fear that it might later be discoverable, which could lead to retribution by paramilitary groups. Strict disclosure rules and internal security procedures with respect to the handling of tapes should ameliorate this fear.

[24]SACHR is the government-appointed board which advises the government on human rights concerns.

[25]Helsinki Watch, *Human Rights in Northern Ireland*, pp. 34-35.

[26]Northern Ireland Office, press release, January 10, 1996.

the silent picture defies any possibility of drawing meaningful conclusions about what is being said by way of question and answer."[27]

- **Confessions:** Under section 12 of the EPA, confessions are admissible unless the defense presents *prima facie* evidence that the accused was subjected to "torture, to inhuman or degrading treatment, or to any violence or threat of violence (whether or not amounting to torture), in order to induce [an accused] to make the statement." The prosecution must disprove this defense beyond a reasonable doubt. The Lawyers Committee for Human Rights has argued that "this standard means that physical deprivation or psychological pressure short of outright violence is permissible. It also means that nothing prevents the introduction of involuntary confessions. This test, moreover, remains in tandem with the obvious problems a defendant faces in obtaining evidence of coercion in a setting where the only others present are the ones who would have the opportunity and the incentive to coerce a confession in the first place."[28] In the absence of audio and video recording, coupled with the denial of counsel in interrogations, the ability of a detainee to obtain *prima facie* evidence of violent coercion is seriously undermined.

- **Legal Advice Unit:** Under the current legal aid scheme in Northern Ireland, detainees choose their own attorneys who may apply for legal aid fees to fund the representation. In 1994, the Independent Commissioner for the Holding Centres proposed the establishment of a legal advice unit managed and operated by the Law Society of Northern Ireland and funded by the government.[29] Detainees were to have immediate access to counsel, but the government would fund such counsel only if the detainee chose representation from the legal advice unit of lawyers associated with the holding center. The Independent Commissioner argued that an on-site unit would prevent undue delays in access to counsel. Opponents argued

---

[27]*Fourth Annual (1996) Report*, p. 32.

[28]Lawyers Committee for Human Rights, *At the Crossroads: Human Rights and the Northern Ireland Peace Process* (New York: LCHR, October 1996), p. 121.

[29]Independent Commissioner for the Holding Centres, *Delayed Choice or Instant Access? Legal Advice for Detainees in Holding Centres* (Belfast: ICHC, November 1994). The Law Society is the professional association for solicitors (lawyers) in Northern Ireland.

inter alia that the right to counsel was two-fold under international standards: prompt access coupled with counsel of one's choice.[30] The Law Society firmly rejected the Independent Commissioner's proposal.[31] Despite assurances that the proposal had been scrapped,[32] the Independent Commissioner's most recent report gives Human Rights Watch/Helsinki cause for serious concern. In response to the European Court of Human Rights decision in *Murray v. U.K.*, the Independent Commissioner argues that an on-site lawyer could immediately brief a detainee on the implications of remaining silent: "any other solution to meet the situation posed by *Murray* would be less than satisfactory."[33] Currently, the Independent Commissioner is encouraging the Law Society to "review its hardened position...and contemplate establishing a pilot project" at Gough Barracks.[34] Human Rights Watch/Helsinki remains in strong opposition to the proposal because it is a regressive measure which will further erode confidence in Northern Ireland's legal system. In fact, no solution to the problem posed by *Murray* would be satisfactory without the full restoration of the common law right to silence or the implementation of a policy delaying the interrogation of a detainee until she or he has had access to counsel.

---

[30]Lawyers Committee for Human Rights, *Choice Without Delay: Interrogation, Legal Advice, and Human Rights in Northern Ireland* (New York: LCHR, September 1995). The United Nations Basic Principles on the Role of Lawyers states that "All persons are entitled to call upon the assistance of a lawyer of their choice to protect and establish their rights and to defend them in all stages of criminal proceedings." Eighth United Nations Congress on the Prevention of Crime and the Treatment of Offenders, Havana, August 27 to September 7, 1990, U.N. Doc. A/CONF.144/28/Rev.1 at 118 (1990), principle 1.

[31]Human Rights Watch/Helsinki interview with Michael Davey, Richard Montieth, and Tony Caher of the Law Society of Northern Ireland, Belfast, November 14, 1996.

[32]Human Rights Watch/Helsinki interview with Trevor French, Chief Executive of the ICHC, Belfast, November 8, 1996.

[33]*Fourth Annual (1996) Report*, p. 44.

[34]Ibid., p. 47.

Police Accountability

There is a tripartite administrative structure responsible for policing in Northern Ireland which rests on the inter-relationship of the secretary of state, the Police Authority for Northern Ireland (PANI),[35] and the chief constable of the RUC. Police complaints procedures involve primarily the RUC and the Independent Commission for Police Complaints (ICPC).[36] Since 1994, there has been a series of reviews, consultations and evaluations related to the reform of policing in Northern Ireland and the need for greater public accountability.[37] In light of issues discussed in this report—severe international criticism of the substance and operation of the emergency regime, the serious widespread violence that accompanied the summer 1996 marching season, the marked rise in

---

[35]PANI is the civilian oversight board responsible for presenting the views of the community to the government and the RUC.

[36]ICPC is the government-appointed civilian body responsible for receiving (along with the RUC) complaints against the police and supervising the investigation of complaints.

[37]See Royal Ulster Constabulary, *A Fundamental Review of Policing: Summary and Key Findings* (Belfast: RUC, January 1997). This review was a joint project involving the RUC, the government, and the Police Authority. According to the summary, the cease-fire period offered state authorities responsible for policing in Northern Ireland "an opportunity to conduct a fundamental review of policing to determine...the nature, level, and style of policing service which would be appropriate in an environment free from the threat of terrorism and sectarian threat." The summary makes quite clear, however, that many of the "key findings" in the review are "security dependent" and cannot be implemented in the current security climate in Northern Ireland. Thus, the review falls into the same trap as Lord Lloyd's inquiry into the emergency legislation: it predicates its findings on a hypothetical peace as opposed to viewing police reform as a confidence-building measure contributing to the advancement of peace. See also Northern Ireland Office, *Foundations for Policing: Proposals for Policing Structures in Northern Ireland (White Paper)* (London: HMSO, May 1996); Police Authority for Northern Ireland, *"Everyone's Police" A Partnership for Change: A Report on a Community Consultation Undertaken by the Police Authority for Northern Ireland in 1995* (Belfast: PANI, 1996); Labour Party, *Policing in Northern Ireland: A Service for All People (A Labour Party Consultation Paper)*, April 1996. The complaints procedure has also been evaluated and proposals have been put forth for its reform. See Dr. Maurice Hayes, *A Police Ombudsman for Northern Ireland? A Review of the Police Complaints System in Northern Ireland*, (London: Northern Ireland Office, January 1997); Independent Commission for Police Complaints for Northern Ireland, *Triennial Review 1994-1997* (London: HMSO, January 1997).

punishment assaults, and ongoing allegations of security force collusion in loyalist paramilitary activities—the need for police reform is a matter urgency.

Human Rights Watch/Helsinki is particularly concerned that under the current structure, there is little accountability for the decisions and conduct of the RUC. A sample of the problems we encountered and discussed in meetings with the government, the Police Authority, the Independent Commission for Police Complaints, and the RUC includes:

• **Independence:** While the Police Authority and the Independent Commission for Police Complaints claim that they are independent bodies separate from the government and the police, all their members are appointed by the Northern Ireland secretary of state. The Police Authority particularly is widely perceived to be merely an extension of the secretary of state's role in policing thus severely undermining the principle of independent civilian oversight.

• **Accountability:** There is no formal requirement that the RUC answer to the government. Although the chief constable is supposed to be accountable to the Police Authority, there has been considerable tension between the RUC and the authority with respect to the chief constable's accountability, especially since the Police Authority has no say in police operational matters. It appears also that responsibility for security policing is exclusively within the domain of the secretary of state and the RUC. The Police Authority *de facto* does not participate in the consideration of policing issues related to special police powers under the emergency legislation. Thus, security policies and police operations fail to take into account the impact of the emergency regime—or any operational decision such as those taken by the police during the 1996 marching season—on the community. According to Police Authority member Professor Herbie Wallace, the authority has no input when it comes to the "operational independence" of the RUC but "we can ask for an explanation afterward."[38]

• **Complaints:** Currently, complaints against the police can be lodged either directly with the RUC or through the Independent Commission for Police Complaints. The commission cannot initiate investigations but can supervise the investigation of complaints referred to it by the RUC, the

---

[38]Human Rights Watch/Helsinki interview, Belfast, November 11, 1996.

secretary of state, and the Police Authority. The RUC is responsible for conducting the investigation. The problem of the police investigating the police is self-evident. In 1995, the complaints commission considered 1,373 cases for disciplinary action, involving 2,385 separate allegations. Of the total number of cases, 1,061 were referred by the police to the director of public prosecutions (DPP). The DPP directed fourteen criminal charges. In only sixteen cases, involving twenty-two separate charges, were formal disciplinary charges leveled against offending officers in 1995. Of the twenty-two charges, only five were substantiated.[39] Of 234 allegations against police officers by persons arrested under the emergency legislation, no officer was found guilty of a breach of discipline.[40] In January 1997, Dr. Maurice Hayes, the government-appointed independent reviewer of the police complaints system, recommended the appointment of a police ombudsman for Northern Ireland who would receive all complaints against police officers first and decide how such complaints would be handled, including the investigation of complaints. In cases of deaths in police custody or under pursuit, allegations of serious assault by a police officer or other serious abuse of power, the ombudsman would be required to conduct an independent investigation.[41] Following the Labour Party's electoral victory in May 1997, these recommendations must now be considered by the new secretary of state for Northern Ireland, Dr. Marjorie Mowlam.

Composition of the RUC

Police accountability within some of the communities served by the RUC is severely hampered by the composition of the force. According to the 1991 census, the population of Northern Ireland is 1,577,836. Approximately 50 percent of the population is Protestant and 38 percent is Catholic.[42]

---

[39]Independent Commission for Police Complaints, *Annual Report 1995* (London: HMSO, May 1, 1996), Table V, p. 51.

[40]Ibid., Table VII, p. 54.

[41]Hayes, *A Police Ombudsman for Northern Ireland?*, p. vi.

[42]Of 1,577,836 people, 605,639 registered their religion as Catholic on census forms; 798,136 registered their religion as Protestant. 174,063 registered "no religion" or did not state any religious affiliation.

These proportions are not reflected in the composition of the RUC. According to RUC statistics for 1996, 88.67 percent of regular officers and 88.12 percent of full-time reserve officers are Protestant. Catholic officers comprise 8.16 percent of regular officers and 6.49 percent of full-time reserve officers. Part-time reserve officers are 93.62 percent Protestant and 5.02 percent Catholic respectively. These percentages have not varied by more than one percent in any category since 1991.[43]

Statistics for recruits are marginally better. In 1996, 76.11 percent of regular recruits and 73.08 percent of full-time reserve recruits were Protestant. Catholics represented 15.93 percent of regular recruits and 15.38 percent of full-time reserve recruits. The percentage of Catholic recruits rose 4 percent from 1995 to 1996 in the regular force and more than doubled from 1995 to 1996 in the full-time reserve force.[44] There has been a 9.3 percent increase in Catholic regular recruits from 1994 to 1996.[45] There was no recruiting undertaken in 1996 in the part-time reserve forces, but Catholic recruits were 9 and 10 percent in 1994 and 1995 respectively.[46]

It is also instructive to review the actual numbers of Catholic applicants offered positions on the police force. For example, in 1992, Catholics comprised 231 of the 2,317 applicants for positions. The RUC accepted a total of 326 applicants. Only twenty-six of those accepted were Catholic. In 1993, eighty-six of 733 applicants were Catholic. Out of sixty-five applicants accepted, only three were Catholic. There were 5,999 applicants—954 of them Catholic—in 1994, a dramatic increase over 1993. Of 187 acceptances, twenty-six were Catholic

---

[43]Letter from RUC Chief Constable Ronnie Flanagan to Human Rights Watch/Helsinki, Table 15, March 7, 1997.

[44]Ibid. Catholic regular recruits rose from 11.76 percent in 1995 to 15.93 percent in 1996 and Catholic full-time reserve recruits rose from 6.82 percent in 1995 to 15.38 percent in 1996. The most dramatic rise in Catholic regular recruits was from 1994 to 1995 when they went from 6.60 percent to 11.76 percent of all recruits.

[45]Ibid. In 1994, Catholic regular recruits were 6.6 percent.

[46]Ibid.

applicants. In 1995, 906 out of 4,458 applicants were Catholic. Of 223 acceptances, thirty-five were Catholic.[47]

The imbalance in religious representation on the force has been acknowledged by the Police Authority and the RUC. On October 18, 1994, the authority requested that the RUC chief constable submit a report on the measures being taken to redress religious imbalance in the force. It then recommended that the RUC establish a "working party" to consider how best to progress the aim of achieving religious balance.[48] RUC Chief Constable Ronnie Flanagan told Human Rights Watch/Helsinki that republican paramilitary threats were "a major stumbling block" to recruiting Catholics but that the RUC acknowledged the problem:

> There is a major threat from the IRA to new recruits and their families. There is also a class dimension. It is difficult to recruit from West Belfast. However, during the cessation of violence, applications from Catholics leapt from 12 percent to 22 percent. After the end of the cease-fire, it went back down to 16 percent. But we realize that it's not enough to say, "Oh, it's a threat." We must take positive action to encourage under-represented groups to apply.[49]

A religious imbalance of the proportions represented above—in the context of the Northern Ireland conflict—presents a profound challenge to RUC claims of impartiality. Human Rights Watch/Helsinki urges the government of the United Kingdom, the RUC and the Police Authority to take immediate steps to redress the imbalance in order to demonstrate that the RUC is representative of the entire community.

---

[47]These figures are from the on-line edition of the Hansard Index which provides information about debates in the House of Commons. The figures were provided by Baroness Denton of Wakefield, the parliamentary under-secretary of state for Northern Ireland, on December 12, 1996.

[48]Police Authority for Northern Ireland, *"Everyone's Police,"* para. 5.5.8.

[49]Human Rights Watch/Helsinki interview, Belfast, November 11, 1996. Note that the chief constable refers here only to the percentage of Catholic applicants not the percentage of those Catholic applicants offered positions on the force.

4. THE POLICING OF PARADES AND MARCHES

Introduction

The violence that erupted in the summer of 1996 marked the worst episode of civil unrest in Northern Ireland since the hunger strikes of the early 1980s.[50] In July 1996 two men were killed, hundreds of people suffered physical injuries, access to the international airport was severely curtailed, civilian roadblocks seriously impeded movement, and damage to property ran into millions of pounds sterling. By all accounts, there was a serious breakdown in the rule of law resulting in grave consequences for the administration of justice in Northern Ireland.

The apparent context for these disturbances was the ongoing dispute between loyalist fraternal orders and local communities organized in strong opposition to loyalist marches through predominantly nationalist areas.[51] The fraternal orders portray their processions as traditional marches giving expression to their religious and cultural heritage, and argue that their right to free assembly

---

[50]In October 1980, republican prisoners in the H-Blocks of Long Kesh Prison began a hunger strike in pursuit of their demand for status as political prisoners. In May 1981, hunger strikers Bobby Sands and Francis Hughes died. (Sands had been elected an MP for Fermanagh/South Tyrone in April 1981, while on hunger strike.) The strikers' deaths gave rise to serious rioting across Northern Ireland and in Dublin. Ten prisoners died before the strike ended in October 1981. Tim Pat Coogan, *The Troubles: Ireland's Ordeal 1966-1996 and the Search for Peace* (Boulder: Roberts Rhinehart Publishers, 1996), p. 194. See also David Beresford, *Ten Men Dead* (London: Grafton, 1987).

[51]This report is confined to the policing of marches and parades in the summer of 1996. For a history of parading and the effect of disputed parades on community relations see Neil Jarman and Dominic Bryan, *Parade and Protest: A Discussion of Parading Disputes in Northern Ireland* (University of Ulster: Centre for the Study of Conflict, 1996). The authors confirm that:

> The history of the north of Ireland over the last two hundred years is littered with incidents of civil disturbances connected to parades. The intercommunal disturbances of 1969, that marked the start of the current version of what is known as 'the Troubles,' were often sparked off by parades and demonstrations. Since then parades and demonstrations running each year from Easter right through to September, 'the marching season,' annually raise tensions and require a massive amount of policing.

Ibid., p. 1.

is unduly infringed by nationalist opposition.[52] They also claim that many march routes originally were populated predominantly by unionists[53] and that shifting demographics do not make the routes any less traditional.[54] Nationalist groups characterize the marches as sectarian, providing the traditionally privileged unionists with a forum in which to re-enact historic triumphs of Protestants over Catholics, often to the point of inciting hatred. They also argue that the heavy police presence accompanying the marches, characterized by intimidating operational tactics, disproportionately disrupts the life of nationalist communities.[55] Attempts at accommodation between residents and marchers routinely failed in the run-up to the 1996 marching season as the loyal orders asserted their "right to march" where and when they wanted and many residents' groups demanded a "right to consent" to marches proceeding through their communities.

To cast the summer's events simply as a matter of intercommunal conflict, however, fails to address the responsibility of state authorities in Northern Ireland to maintain the rule of law, thus assuring both communities equal protection of

---

[52]The fraternal orders that organize marches and parades include: the Orange Order, the largest and most politically influential of the orders; the Royal Black Institution, an order professing a more religious focus; and the Apprentice Boys of Derry, which holds parades commemorating the closing of the city gates by the apprentice boys during the Siege of Derry in 1688. There is considerable overlap in membership among these groups. For example, membership in the Orange Order is a prerequisite for membership in the Royal Black Institution. Although the Apprentice Boys is a separate group, many members also hold membership in the Orange Order. Jarman and Bryan, *Parade and Protest*, pp. 6-13.

[53]The words "loyal" and "loyalist" are used here to describe the fraternal orders themselves but "unionist" is used generally to refer to the community of Protestants who support the orders and the maintenance of the union of Northern Ireland with the United Kingdom. In some testimony, interviewees use "loyalist" and "unionist" interchangeably.

[54]Human Rights Watch/Helsinki met with representatives of all three orders. Interviews were conducted with: Alistair Simpson and William Moore, Apprentice Boys of Derry, London/Derry, November 7, 1996; William Logan and William Abernethy, Royal Black Institution, Belfast, November 14, 1996; Rev. Martin Smyth, Orange Order, Belfast, November 18, 1996.

[55]Both nationalists and unionists hold parades and marches. The vast majority of parades are sponsored by loyalist fraternal orders. In 1995, 3,500 parades and marches were held in Northern Ireland. According to the RUC, 2,581 marches were loyalist and 302 were nationalist; 617 were described as "other" and twenty-four were categorized "illegal." *The Chief Constable's Annual Report: Royal Ulster Constabulary 1995*, June 1996, p. 21.

their rights. The marching season of 1996 must be placed in a broader context which recognizes and confronts the grievous failure of the police, state agencies invested with responsibility for the oversight of policing, and the government of the United Kingdom, to prevent the collapse of law and order. Despite RUC claims of being caught in the middle of disputes between nationalists and unionists over the "right to march,"[56] a series of police actions—sanctioned by the government— exacerbated the conflict resulting in the effective submission of state authorities to the threat of unionist violence, the use of excessive force against peaceful demonstrators, the indiscriminate use of life-threatening plastic bullets[57] against both unionist and nationalist protesters, and a general failure to halt illegal activities such as the blockade of the airport and the establishment of illegal roadblocks. State authorities are responsible for the summer's events by acts of omission and acts of commission.

Police actions during the summer of 1996 led to a serious crisis in public confidence in the police force. The Committee on the Administration of Justice commented that these actions "have all contributed to significant sections of Northern Ireland society questioning whether the state and its agencies are able or willing to give concrete expression to the rule of law."[58] The Standing Advisory Commission on Human Rights (SACHR) called for an independent inquiry into the summer's events, stating publicly:

> The Commission considers that the failure to maintain the supremacy of the rule of law during this period has resulted in

---

[56]Then RUC Chief Constable Sir Hugh Annesley stated that he wanted the government to look into the issue of how parades and demonstrations are run in Northern Ireland "and how they can be reconciled between the two sides, because...I am sick to death of being stuck in the middle of a non-winnable situation." See David Sharrock, "Ulster on Alert for Backlash," *The Guardian*, July 12, 1996.

[57]Plastic bullets are also referred to as plastic baton rounds. There is a separate section in this report which details the history of the use of plastic bullets in Northern Ireland, criticism of their accuracy, the number of people who have been killed by them, and a critique of their use during the summer 1996 marching season. See pp. 72-82 herein.

[58]Committee on the Administration of Justice, *The Misrule of Law: A Report on the Policing of Events During the Summer of 1996 in Northern Ireland* (Belfast: CAJ, October 1996), p. 2. CAJ is a Belfast-based, cross-community human rights organization which organized teams of independent observers to monitor the summer 1996 marching events.

widespread abuse of human rights. The Commission is firmly of the view that the failure to set up a comprehensive inquiry will make it almost impossible to restore the confidence in and acceptance of the institutions of the State which are essential for a just and stable society.[59]

The government of the United Kingdom failed to establish an independent inquiry. In late July 1996, the secretary of state for Northern Ireland, Sir Patrick Mayhew, established a general review body to evaluate the "current arrangements for handling public processions and open-air public meetings and associated public order issues in Northern Ireland."[60] Mayhew also requested that the annual review by Her Majesty's Inspectorate of Constabulary (HMIC) include an evaluation of plastic bullet use during the summer of 1996.[61] While the recommendations resulting from these inquiries failed to address adequately the core elements responsible for the breakdown in the rule of law, the appointments of HMIC and the review body clearly signaled the government's recognition that the summer's events led to a level of violence which threatened to destabilize efforts to bring peace to Northern Ireland. It is Human Rights Watch/Helsinki's hope that the government will take responsibility for its own role, and the role of state policing agencies, in creating the environment within which last summer's violence occurred.

Public Order Legislation in Northern Ireland
The domestic law governing public processions in Northern Ireland is the Public Order (Northern Ireland) Order 1987.[62] The order sets forth requirements for those wishing to hold a parade or march and enumerates powers granted to the police and the government with respect to public processions. This discussion focuses on specific provisions of the legislation in force in 1996 and thus governing

---

[59]Standing Advisory Commission on Human Rights, press release, August 8, 1996.

[60]Northern Ireland Office, press release, "Review of Parades and Marches in Northern Ireland: Terms of Reference," July 24, 1996. (See also section below titled "Independent Review of Parades and Marches.")

[61]Northern Ireland Office, press release, "Review of the Use of Plastic Baton Rounds," July 24, 1996. (See also section below titled "Plastic Bullets.")

[62]*Public Order (Northern Ireland) Order 1987*, No. 463 (N.I. 7).

the summer 1996 marching season. The domestic legal regime governing marches is reviewed and critiqued here to facilitate an understanding of the authority for policing decisions taken with respect to the events described in this report.

Article 3 of the order requires organizers of a public procession to give the police written notice of the date, time, route and number of participants within seven days of the event. If seven days notice is "not reasonably practicable," notice can be given at a later date thus allowing for spontaneous demonstrations and counter-demonstrations.[63]

The RUC retains significant decision-making powers under the legislation, including the power to impose conditions such as rerouting, if public order is threatened. Article 4 states:

> 4.-(1) If a senior police officer, having regard to the time or place at which and the circumstances in which any public procession is being held or is intended to be held and to its route or proposed route, reasonably believes that-
>
>> (a) it may result in serious public disorder, serious damage to property or serious disruption to the life of the community; or
>>
>> (b) the purpose of the persons organising it is the intimidation of others with a view to compelling them not to do an act they have a right to do, or to do an act they have a right not to do,
>
> he may give directions imposing on the persons organising or taking part in the procession such conditions as appear to him necessary to prevent such disorder, damage, disruption or intimidation, including conditions as to the route of the procession or prohibiting it from entering any place specified in the directions.

If a senior police officer reasonably believes that (a) or (b) above might occur, under article 4(2) he may also

> give directions imposing on the persons organising or taking part in the meeting such conditions as to the place at which the

---

[63]In May 1997, the new government amended the Public Order order. (See section below titled "Independent Review of Parades and Marches".) The notice requirement has been changed to twenty-one days and alcohol is now banned at all marches and parades.

meeting may be (or continue to be) held, its maximum duration, or the maximum number of persons who may constitute it, as appear necessary to him to prevent such disorder, damage, disruption or intimidation.

Police powers are not limited to those enumerated. An RUC senior officer can impose any "such conditions as appear to him necessary" to prevent disorder. Theoretically, the imposition of conditions by the police (or lack thereof) can be challenged by march organizers or residents through the process of judicial review. The courts in Northern Ireland, however, have proven reluctant to interfere with police operational decisions unless the senior officer has ignored statutory criteria or has reached what the court determines is a demonstrably unreasonable decision. The judiciary appears to have adopted a uniform position to remain uninvolved in the phenomenon of contentious marches, and it is rare for an application for judicial review related to marches or parades to succeed.[64]

---

[64]The judgment of the Northern Ireland Court of Appeal in *In the Matter of an Application by Conor Murphy for Judicial Review* set the tone for the judiciary's response to contentious marches. In 1991, the RUC allowed an Orange Order march through the predominantly nationalist village of Pomeroy, County Tyrone. The residents filed an application for judicial review of the police decision not to reroute the march. The lower court judge held that the RUC had not taken account of the likelihood of extensive disruption to the community and referred the case back to the RUC. On appeal, the court held that it had not been proven that the RUC failed to give adequate consideration to the statutory criteria. Lord Chief Justice Hutton's ruling served as the precedent to which the Northern Ireland courts remain firmly committed:

> The governing principle...is that the court does not sit as a Court of Appeal to substitute its opinion of what should be the proper decision of the person or body entrusted by Parliament with the making of the decision...There may be arguments of weight and substance on both sides of the matter, but it is not for the court to weigh up the arguments for and against the decision. The weighing of these arguments is a matter for the decision maker, not for the court.

In the Matter of an Application by Conor Murphy for Judicial Review, (1991) 5 N.I.J.B. 88. Cited in Tom Hadden and Anne Donnelly, *The Legal Control of Marches in Northern Ireland: A Report to the Community Relations Council* (Queen's University of Belfast: Centre for International and Comparative Human Rights Law, January 1997), pp. 26-27. British Irish Rights Watch, a London-based human rights group, has labeled this approach "a dereliction of duty" by the judiciary to uphold the rule of law in situations where the RUC does not exercise its decision-making power properly, thus failing to protect the rights of both communities. British Irish Rights Watch, *Submission to the Independent Review of*

The secretary of state for Northern Ireland, in consultation with the RUC chief constable and, "wherever practicable" with the Police Authority, alone has the power to ban a march or parade. The secretary of state may make an order prohibiting a public procession if conditions imposed by the police under article 4 are insufficient to prevent "disorder, damage, disruption or intimidation;" or

> 5.-(1) (b) the holding in any area or place of any public procession or any open-air public meeting is likely to cause-
> (I)   serious public disorder;
> (ii) serious disruption to the life of the community; or
> (iii) undue demands to be made upon the police or military forces.

The power to ban is absolute and not subject to judicial review. According to article 5(3), the secretary of state's "opinion and the information upon which that opinion was formed shall be conclusive evidence of the matters stated therein." The secretary of state's decision to ban is thus not reviewable even if his facts are wrong or if the "outcomes he envisages are unlikely to transpire."[65]

A series of public order offenses are created under articles 9 to 22, including the intentional or likely stirring up of hatred or arousal of fear through words or behavior or the publication or distribution of threatening or abusive written material. Additional offenses include riotous or disorderly behavior, provocative conduct, obstructive sitting, and carrying an offensive weapon in a public place.

The Public Order (Northern Ireland) Order has been criticized primarily for the dual role in which it places the police with respect to contentious parades and marches. The police are responsible not only for making decisions about the conditions under which marches proceed, they are responsible also for enforcing their decisions. The RUC also has been criticized for unreasonable delay in making decisions on rerouting or the imposition of other conditions on marches. Critics argue:

> Waiting until the last minute before announcing whether a parade is to go ahead or not inevitably leads to an increase in

---

Parades and Marches, October 1996, p. 12.

[65]British Irish Rights Watch, *Submission to the Independent Review of Parades and Marches*, p. 3.

tension and confusion both amongst marchers and those opposed to the march. It often appears that the police tactic is to wait until the last minute to determine who appears likely to cause the most disruption if the decision goes against them—in other words, who can assemble the largest number of supporters. This is clearly not an appropriate way to exercise the powers afforded to the police in the Public Order Order.[66]

The exercise of police powers under the order should not be a simple consideration of which side can demonstrate the greater show of force. According to this calculus, one group threatens the police with massive public disorder if it does not get a favorable decision. The real possibility in Northern Ireland of carrying out this threat creates an environment in which mob rule is rewarded with a decision by the RUC favorable to the threatening group. Such decisions are then justified by the police as taken in the interest of maintaining public order, preserving life and protecting property. The RUC tactic of delaying decisions to the last moment contributes to creating the very conditions of threat it claims to be avoiding. This "wait and see" strategy makes the RUC beholden to whichever group strategically uses the time allotted to gather the numbers necessary to create a credible threat. RUC delays—wittingly or unwittingly—create the conditions which allow the threat of one group to become a decisive factor in its own decision-making process.

The circumstances of life in Northern Ireland, characterized by the divisions between the nationalist and unionist communities, require more active consideration of the other relevant criteria provided by the public order legislation, such as serious disruption to the life of the community. The RUC's single focus on serious public disorder, in the context of the conflict in Northern Ireland, is a recipe for hardening community divisions thus making the police a partner in the perpetuation of violence.

The Standoff at Drumcree: July 7 to 11, 1996
On Saturday, July 6, 1996, the RUC notified the Orange Order that a march scheduled to proceed from Drumcree Church the following day would be rerouted away from the Garvaghy Road, a predominantly Catholic nationalist area

---

[66]Committee on the Administration of Justice, *The Misrule of Law*, pp. 54-55.

in Portadown.[67] This decision was taken after attempts at accommodation between the residents of Garvaghy Road and the Portadown District Lodge of the Orange Order failed. RUC management clearly perceived a major threat of violence if the march was not rerouted.[68]

On Sunday, July 7, 1996, Orangemen began to converge on Drumcree and commenced a stand-off with the police, who by then had called in backup support from the British army. The Orangemen demanded to march down the Garvaghy Road and threatened to stand against the police until their demand was met. By the end of the day, an estimated 5,000 Orangemen and unionists in support of the Orange Order had gathered at Drumcree. A report by three Labour Party TDs[69]

---

[67]In addition to personal testimony, Human Rights Watch/Helsinki relied on a number of chronologies of the events of summer 1996 for this report: *Report of the Independent Review of Parades and Marches* (Belfast: The Stationary Office, January 1997), pp. 34-38 (this is the final report of the body established by Sir Patrick Mayhew to address the future handling of public processions); Committee on the Administration of Justice, *The Misrule of Law*, Appendix II, pp. 79-86; British Irish Rights Watch, "Chronology of Disturbances in Northern Ireland July and August 1996," September 1996; Pat Finucane Centre, *In the Line of Fire: Derry July 1996* (London/Derry: PFC, August 1996), pp. 10-13.

[68]The rationale for the original decision by the RUC to reroute the march has been much debated. Brendan McAllister of the Mediation Network of Northern Ireland understood the decision as compliance with an agreement struck by the network with the RUC prior to an Orange Order march scheduled to proceed down the Garvaghy Road in July 1995. McAllister claims that then Deputy Chief Constable Ronnie Flanagan (now RUC chief constable) told him there would be no march in 1996 without the consent of the residents if the 1995 march were permitted to proceed without incident. McAllister brought this "point of understanding" back to the Garvaghy Road residents and the Orange Order march proceeded in 1995. Human Rights Watch/Helsinki interview with Brendan McAllister, Belfast, November 11, 1996. Ronnie Flanagan denies that such a bargain was ever struck. He told Human Rights Watch/Helsinki that the decision to reroute the 1996 Orange Order march was taken strictly in order "to avoid outright sectarian violence, community on community." Human Rights Watch/Helsinki interview, Belfast, November 11, 1996. Other attempts at accommodation failed as well. For example, Orange Order representatives refused to meet with the Garvaghy Road Residents Coalition (GRRC) because its chairperson, Brendan MacCionnaith, is a former republican prisoner. Human Rights Watch/Helsinki interview with Brendan MacCionnaith, Portadown, November 17, 1996.

[69]The Irish word for "member of parliament" is "teachta dáil" and is abbreviated as TD.

from the Republic of Ireland who served as observers at Drumcree described the scene:

> On Sunday morning [July 7] the area around the Church of Ireland Church at Drumcree and its Roman Catholic graveyard resembled a battlefield. Razor wire was stretched along the fields and meadows; armoured vehicles positioned on the bridge blocked the road leading from Drumcree Church to the Garvaghy Road; RUC in full riot gear and fully armed were deployed behind their vehicles and in the surrounding fields and laneways. The army was deployed further back in a second line of defense. It was a strong position.[70]

The stand-off lasted for four and one-half days. In the period from July 7 to 11, 1996, unionist protests against the police decision to reroute the march broke out across Northern Ireland resulting in a serious crisis in public order. Many of these protest actions were illegal and some were violent:

• Unionist protesters established and manned numerous roadblocks, severely impeding movement across Northern Ireland. Protesters blocked access to roads leading to Belfast's international airport effectively shutting it down.[71]

• An armored vehicle was stolen by unionists and conveyed to Drumcree where it remained throughout the stand-off. A number of vehicles were hijacked.[72]

---

[70]Deputy Declan Bree, Deputy Joe Costello and Senator Sean Maloney, *Report by Labour Parliamentary Group of Observers at Drumcree, Lr. Ormeau Road and Derry*, July 16, 1996, p.1.

[71]Michael O'Toole and Fabian Boyle, "Diary of a Day Filled with Violent Incidents," *Irish News*, July 9, 1996.

[72]Ibid. This vehicle is referred to as a "digger" in some testimony.

- The Housing Executive reported numerous applications for emergency housing from Catholics forced to evacuate their homes under threat of violence from unionist protesters.[73]

- Property damage, losses to businesses, and a virtual halt in tourism resulted in the loss of tens of millions pounds sterling.[74]

- On July 11, 1996, the RUC reported 758 attacks on the police with sixty-five officers injured.[75]

Although the overwhelming majority of plastic bullets fired in July 1996 were directed at the nationalist community (see section below titled "Plastic Bullets"), some unionists complained about indiscriminate and excessive plastic baton round use during the Drumcree stand-off:

- Yvonne Robinson, a resident of Portadown's unionist Brownstone housing estate, called for a ban on plastic bullets after her nineteen-year-old, mentally disabled son, Daniel, was hit in the chest and critically wounded when disturbances erupted between police and unionist protesters at Drumcree on July 8, 1996. Daniel Robinson's spleen was ruptured and he suffered lung damage. Mrs. Robinson noted that, despite the RUC's mandate to "aim low," Daniel had been shot in the chest.[76]

- John Taylor, deputy leader of the Ulster Unionist Party (UUP), charged the RUC with shooting plastic bullets "at random." He stated, "Some members of the RUC are quite trigger-happy. I'm sure RUC officers have been attacked. I'm not sure any have been attacked at Drumcree. The RUC are not applying the principle of the minimum use of force."[77]

---

[73]*Report of the Independent Review of Parades and Marches*, p. 39.

[74]Ibid., pp. 38-39.

[75]David McKittrick, "The Present is Orange," *The Independent*, July 12, 1996.

[76]Stephanie Bell, "Mum Calls for Plastic Bullet Ban," *Sunday Life*, July 14, 1996.

[77]Brenda O'Neill, "Nearly 100 Arrests due to Violence," *Irish News*, July 11, 1996.

At the beginning of the stand-off, 2,000 police officers were deployed as reinforcements to Portadown. Despite the use of plastic baton rounds in some instances, the massive police and army presence, and the quasi-military geography of the police operation at Drumcree itself, the RUC appeared reluctant to intervene to halt many of the illegal activities which allowed the mass of protesters at Drumcree to grow to an estimated 10,000 by the end of the week. Eamon Stack of the Garvaghy Road Residents Coalition told Human Rights Watch/Helsinki:

> Drumcree was an illegal demonstration. But the RUC never tried
> to keep people from coming. There were attacks on the RUC.
> The rest of the town was completely under the control of the
> Orange Order. Orangemen were allowed to walk about freely.
> They drove in cars with Union Jacks. The Orange men actually
> gave policemen's names out over the loudspeakers. The people
> here saw no action by the RUC to prevent the illegal activity that
> was going on. When the RUC left, they had to go through
> roadblocks manned by loyalists. That digger had to be driven
> past the RUC and the British army and was on display at
> Drumcree. At no stage did they attempt to take that digger. It
> was an artificial stand-off.[78]

According to Éamon Ó Cuív, a parliamentary observer from the Republic of Ireland, the police made no attempt to cease the flow of unionist protesters into Portadown and the area around Drumcree Church:

> There's no doubt in my mind that there was no effort to stop
> people from coming. On Sunday evening, Orangemen were
> directing traffic in and out of Portadown. They were streaming
> in on Sunday evening. We saw the cars. And there was no
> attempt to stop them.[79]

Other members of parliament from the Republic of Ireland who served as observers corroborated this account and charged that the RUC had effectively ceded control of Portadown to the Orange Order:

---

[78]Human Rights Watch/Helsinki interview, Portadown, November 17, 1996.

[79]Human Rights Watch/Helsinki interview, Dublin, November 26, 1996.

That night [Sunday, July 7] as the Labour Group drove out the Moy Road heading for Armagh they encountered no RUC roadblocks. However, they did encounter the Orange Order patrolling the Moy Road and directing traffic in and out of Portadown...[T]he Orange Order controlled access to Drumcree. The RUC were deployed strategically to prevent the Orange Parade through Garvaghy Road but were not deployed to monitor or restrict the movement of the Orange Order into or around Drumcree.[80]

The apparent reluctance of RUC officers to intervene and halt illegal protest activities was widely perceived to be a result of the religious composition of the force and the affiliations of its officers, as well as the fear of reprisals if the police interfered.[81] According to RUC statistics, roughly 90 percent of its officers are Protestant.[82] Furthermore, it has been reported that a large number of RUC officers hold membership in the Orange Order or one of the other fraternal orders.[83] In January 1996 an officer appealed a decision by the RUC to punish him for marching with the Orange Order and the Apprentice Boys. The court held that the RUC could place certain restrictions on the private activities of its officers in order

---

[80]Bree, Costello, Maloney, *Report by Labour Parliamentary Group of Observers*, p. 2.

[81]Fear of reprisal was a legitimate concern. Not only were the Orangemen and their supporters involved in violent and illegal protest activities, the reading by Orangemen of individual officers' names over a loudspeaker at Drumcree was understood to be a threat to the police. Human Rights Watch/Helsinki interview with Eamon Stack, Portadown, November 17, 1996. It was also reported that a number of officers were driven out of their homes by threats in the aftermath of the stand-off. *Police Beat*, Newsletter of the Police Federation of Northern Ireland, August 1996.

[82]Letter from RUC Chief Constable Ronnie Flanagan to Human Rights Watch/Helsinki, March 7, 1997.

[83]Ben Webster, "RUC Men Investigated Over Loyalist Parades," *Irish News*, September 5, 1996. RUC officers are not prohibited from belonging to fraternal orders and there is no requirement that officers disclose such membership.

that the RUC be viewed as even-handed.[84] RUC Chief Constable Ronnie Flanagan told Human Rights Watch/Helsinki:

> We concentrate on officers' behavior. We do not look at membership per se. The RUC is currently considering a policy of disclosure where officers declare their memberships openly. But there is a fear of chilling; every officer has freedom of association.[85]

As Orangemen and their supporters continued to engage in illegal and often violent protest activities, charges were leveled against the leadership of the Orange Order and the Ulster Unionist Party, the entire leadership of which holds membership in the Orange Order, for encouraging their members to engage in illegal activities. The Rev. Martin Smyth, then Grand Master of the Orange Order and Ulster Unionist MP for south Belfast, told Human Rights Watch/Helsinki:

> I was accused of calling people out in violent protest. My comments were taken out of context. I was asked at a press conference, "Are you not asking people to break the law?" Throughout history people have had to break the law when a law was unjust; people must be willing to pay the penalty ... Any roadblock is illegal but it's been used as a means of protest by strikers. A permanent blockade would be removed by police immediately. Regularly where strikers use it as a means of

---

[84]Ibid.

[85]Human Rights Watch/Helsinki interview, Belfast, November 11, 1996. The RUC reports that one police officer was charged with a criminal offense for off-duty conduct undertaken during the summer 1996 marching season. Six officers were suspended from duty in connection with their alleged involvement in the events of summer 1996. Four of the six were reported to the director of public prosecutions who directed "no further action" but the disciplinary investigations into their conduct continues. One officer was prosecuted and convicted for "obstruction" and has appealed that decision. It is unclear what action has been taken against the sixth suspended officer. Letter to Human Rights Watch/Helsinki from RUC Chief Superintendent G.W. Sillery, May 12, 1997.

protest, the police would reroute. Roadblocks were always used as a protest mechanism.[86]

The final report of the Independent Review of Parades and Marches, invested with responsibility for evaluating the handling of marches in the aftermath of Drumcree, concluded that many of the roadblocks established by the Orange Order and its supporters "were of a more permanent nature with some lasting for days" and that blocking access to roads was accompanied by "the hijacking and destruction of vehicles, the felling of trees, and other criminal acts, including damage to property."[87] Rev. Smyth's claim that the RUC would be responsible for rerouting traffic away from a "protest" roadblock is untenable. The Orange Order itself put out a call to its members to "stretch the police as much as possible."[88] It is safe to assume that many of the roadblocks were established in response to this call.

In the midst of the stand-off at Drumcree, Michael McGoldrick, a thirty-one-year-old Catholic taxi driver, was killed near Lurgan in County Portadown. It was reported that an Ulster Volunteer Force (UVF) leader in the Portadown/Lurgan area active in organizing unionist protests against the RUC decision to reroute the Orange Order march was responsible for the murder.[89] Although no loyalist paramilitary group actually claimed responsibility for the murder, the killing put the status of the loyalist paramilitary cease-fire in doubt.[90] To date, no one has been charged with Michael McGoldrick's murder.

On Thursday, July 11, then RUC Chief Constable Hugh Annesley reversed the original decision to reroute the Orange Order march away from the

---

[86]Human Rights Watch/Helsinki interview, Belfast, November 18, 1996. Dr. Marjorie Mowlam, the Labour Party's Northern Ireland spokesperson (and in May 1997 named secretary of state for Northern Ireland) explicitly criticized Ulster Unionist Party leaders as "constitutional politicians who had not encouraged their followers to obey the law." Michael White, "Riots 'Defeat for Peace' Admits MP," *The Guardian*, July 16, 1996.

[87]*Report of the Independent Review of Parades and Marches*, January 1997, p.35.

[88]*Belfast Telegraph*, July 9, 1996.

[89]Gerry Moriarty, "Murder Raises Question of Whether Loyalist Ceasefire Can Hold," *Irish Times*, July 9, 1996.

[90]Ibid.

Garvaghy Road. According to press reports, Annesley justified the reversal "by effectively admitting that loyalist violence and the sheer weight of numbers they could command had paid off and the real danger of loss of life had become too high."[91] According to Ronnie Flanagan, current RUC chief constable and one of the RUC's primary strategists at Drumcree:

> By Wednesday, things were getting more dangerous. What options were open to us? We considered a range of options. Had we set-up roadblocks, people would have simply taken to the fields and more fronts would have been created. What would have happened if these numbers overran the police lines? There would have been a shift from policing to military language: "We'd have had to shoot them." There was a very sinister loyalist paramilitary influence. There was a real, imminent, pressing threat to life which was my first priority. Heartbreaking though it was, the question became how to get the thing [the march] down as quickly as possible.[92]

These statements by RUC management strongly suggest that the police succumbed to the Orange Order and its supporters under threat of violence. Sir Patrick Mayhew insisted there had been no political interference in Annesley's reversal and allowing the march to proceed was solely an operational decision.[93] John Steele of the Northern Ireland Office told Human Rights Watch/Helsinki:

> There was no government interference in the decision at Drumcree. Lots of people tell me that they can't believe that because it was such a political moment. The decision was

---

[91]Sharrock, "Ulster on Alert for Backlash," *The Guardian*, July 12, 1996.

[92]Human Rights Watch/Helsinki interview, Belfast, November 11, 1996.

[93]Northern Ireland Office, Speech by Sir Patrick Mayhew, Secretary of State for Northern Ireland, to the Plenary Session of the British-Irish Interparliamentary Body, September 24, 1996. Mayhew stated, "In our constitutional arrangements we hold very firmly to maintaining the operational independence of the RUC. From the inception of the first regular police service over 160 years ago we have never allowed the police...to be the tools of any Ministers."

properly the chief constable's and the secretary of state was kept informed.[94]

According to Ronnie Flanagan, however, "Northern Ireland was at as dangerous a position as at any time in thirty years."[95] It is, therefore, an extraordinary admission by the government of the United Kingdom that it opted out of full participation in any decision involving a crisis in public order of this magnitude. The public order legislation in force in Northern Ireland specifically contemplates situations in which the government, that is, the secretary of state, would be responsible for imposing a political—as opposed to an operational—decision in an attempt to resolve a public order crisis. The government's assertion that it remained uninvolved in the Drumcree reversal despite RUC claims that Northern Ireland was virtually on the brink of civil war begs the question of how extreme a situation must become before the government fulfills its mandate under the Public Order order, particularly when the protection of the minority population of Northern Ireland is at issue.

The Garvaghy Road Residents Coalition had been in contact with both the police and representatives of the Northern Ireland Office during the stand-off.[96] Despite this contact, the decision to allow the Orange Order down the Garvaghy Road was not communicated formally to the residents' group. Brendan MacCionnaith told Human Rights Watch/Helsinki that at 1:00 or 2:00 a.m. on Thursday morning, all the land rovers turned and pointed toward nationalist areas and there was a major redeployment of RUC vehicles. On Thursday morning, July 11, when the Residents Coalition realized the march would proceed, its leadership called for a peaceful demonstration on the Garvaghy Road. Residents sat in the middle of the road and linked arms. According to MacCionnaith:

> The police came in in full riot gear with shields and batons drawn and began pulling people off the road. It was clear from

---

[94]Human Rights Watch/Helsinki interview, Belfast, November 11, 1996.

[95]Human Rights Watch/Helsinki interview, Belfast, November 11, 1996.

[96]According to members of the Residents Coalition, the NIO met with the residents and tried to persuade them to agree to the Orange Order marching down the road in exchange for the establishment of an independent review of parades and marches. The residents declined. Human Rights Watch/Helsinki interview, Portadown, November 17, 1996.

the way they were dressed that the RUC was going to use force. The RUC made no attempt to inform the crowd. The road was cleared of 200-300 people in ten minutes. Some people were trying to get off the road and RUC officers were pushing them back on. There was a wall around the protesters.[97]

Human Rights Watch/Helsinki spoke with dozens of residents about police response to the protest on the Garvaghy Road. According to residents, the first phase of the implementation of the RUC decision to get the march down "as quickly as possible" involved removing protesters from the road. The residents fully expected to be cleared from the road but claim that the RUC unnecessarily batoned people, brutally assaulted a number of protesters, and used throughout the operation sectarian language—slurs based on the presumed Catholicism and nationalist views of the demonstrators:[98]

> **Joe Duffy:** The land rovers were starting to come down the road and form up. I went up to see what was happening and I was hit with a police baton on top of my head. I was stunned blind and pulled behind a land rover and charged with assaulting a police officer. It was an unprovoked attack.
>
> **Rosaleen McNally, age fifty-six:** I said to a lady that the first word to move from the RUC and I would be away. I was scared stiff. All of a sudden all hell broke loose as the police closed in and pushed me from behind with a large shield. The police didn't say a word. I tried to get off the road and on to the footpath [sidewalk] as I panicked but the police kept pushing. I felt a blow to my head from behind and I fell to the ground. My legs were caught by the police walking over me and I was pushed to the right as the police hit out at the people in the next row. I lay there unable to move and put my left arm up to try and protect my head and face and got another blow to my upraised arm. All I could see were RUC boots.

---

[97]Human Rights Watch/Helsinki interview, Portadown, November 17, 1996.

[98]Human Rights Watch/Helsinki interviews, Portadown, November 17, 1996.

Eileen McNally, age thirty-three: I saw Joe Duffy approaching the police. As he began to talk, a policeman drew his baton and began to beat him around the head. As Joe lifted his hands toward his head, the officer continued to hit him while two other officers grabbed him by his arms. I begged another police officer to stop them but he ignored me; he didn't say anything. I couldn't watch it any longer. As I walked away, I met my mother. The police suddenly surrounded everyone. There was a lot of confusion. A line of police formed where I was standing. They then surged into the crowd hitting with their shields. With the force, my mother, my self and Claire Griffin fell to the ground. We were trapped. I got hit on my head, I don't know where it came from; from behind. As I tried to protect my mother, I got hit on my right arm. We were desperately trying to get to our feet, we were terrified. The police were trampling over us to get to people at the front.

John McCook, age forty-four: I was sitting on the road. I was approached by four policemen who proceeded to kick, punch and pull at me. One officer grabbed me by the nose from behind with a knee in my back. One said, "Break the fucker's arm!" because I wouldn't let go of the person next to me. They beat at me with batons. I didn't offer physical resistance. They broke the link with the person on one side then it was easy enough to physically lift me off the road. The assault continued as I was carried off the road. The policemen carrying me would stop intermittently to give me another kick or punch. I was then thrown onto the road in front of Churchill Park and kicked and punched further. Why didn't they read the riot act to give people warning? The police just moved in and that was the end of it.

Katrina Cusack: Three RUC officers grabbed me by the neck and legs and threw me on the foot path. They screamed, "get up off the road you fucking Fenian bastard!"[99] Then one kicked me on the lower back. I was already off the road. As I was getting up, two RUC officers lifted me off my feet and threw me against a land rover face first.

---

[99]"Fenian" is a derogatory term directed against Catholics.

Ruairi Dignam, age eight: I was worried about my mum who was on the road. I was on my way down when an RUC man came around the side of a land rover. He kicked me on the leg very hard. All I was looking for was my mum.

Claire Dignam, age thirty: I was sitting on the road roughly ten minutes. I heard an RUC inspector saying, after lifting his baton over his head, "get into the scum!" I was dragged off the road by the upper part of my body. The officer put his two fingers in my mouth to wrench open my mouth. He pushed his finger and thumbs into my neck under my chin before dragging me off the road. I was thrown on the side of the road. When I got up, another RUC officer in riot gear pushed his shield into my chest and pushed me aside screaming and shouting into my face. When I finally got away from the screaming officer, I seen a person being dragged off the road and he was placed in front of a land rover. The land rover revved up and tried to run over the person. I screamed for people to come over and stop the land rover. It was meant for that land rover to go over him. He would've been dead only I seen him. The RUC officer who placed him there signaled the one in the jeep. I couldn't believe that.

Bernadette Tennyson: They were telling us to go home, calling us "Fenian bastards." They were just disgusting. We had children with us. My wee girl was in hysteria. I witnessed a lady getting beaten by a number of RUC officers. They lifted her and then one RUC officer twisted her arm up her back and another RUC officer was punching her on the middle part of her body. Another RUC officer was beating her around the back with a baton. I was standing just a few feet away.

James Griffin, age sixteen: The police lifted me to a standing position and dragged me to Churchill Park. Both my hands were engaged by two RUC officers. A third came around to my front and smacked me with a baton right across the face. I wasn't trying to get back on the road. As they were dragging me between two land rovers, my head was beaten off the side of one. Only the efforts of my mother and other people pulled me from the hands of the policemen. My nose was broken.

Donna Griffin, mother of James Griffin: To my right hand side I got a glimpse of my son James being led off the road by two policemen; his arm was up his back. As they got to the opening of the two land rovers, one started banging my son's head off the land rover. I pushed forward, grabbed James by his jumper, and with the help of other people got him away from the police. I noticed his nose was bleeding and had already started to swell.

Rita Trainor: I saw my niece Claire Griffin, seventeen years old, being knocked to the footpath by at least ten officers. I went to help her up. At the same time, Mrs. Rosaleen McNally, who is an elderly lady, was knocked down on her face beside us. I was trying to help them to their feet, when I was hit by a baton at the right back of my head. There were only officers behind me. As I rose up another baton hit me on the right upper back of my arm. As I stood to tell the officer a young girl and an elderly lady was on the foot path, the police officer raised his baton to hit me on the face but I got my hand up to cover my face in time so I got the full force on the tips of my open fingers. While all this is going on, the verbal abuse from all the officers was outrageous. They called us "bitch," "cut," and "Fenian bastards." It was very clear to these officers we were not on the road but on the footpath and they continued to beat, push and verbally abuse children, old women and those that tried to help the injured. They were just out of control. It was as if they just wanted to get into you.   The abuse was so horrific that everybody was stunned.

Patrick Skelton, age sixty-nine: I was standing on the edge of the footpath and because I was unable to move, owing to my age, as fast as the police wanted, I was struck with a police shield on the face and pushed very hard down the slope at the edge of the footpath. I was off the road, on the edge of the road. I was in a state of shock for a time afterwards.

The second phase of police response to nationalist protests involved the firing of plastic bullets. (See also section below titled "Plastic Bullets.") Protesters were cleared from the Garvaghy Road and corralled into Churchill Park. Churchill Park faces the Garvaghy Road on one side; the opposite side is enclosed by the building walls of a housing estate. There are narrow alleyways leading from the park into the housing estate.[100] A number of residents protesting on the Garvaghy Road on Thursday, July 11, told Human Rights Watch/Helsinki that as soon as the road was cleared, the police formed a double line of RUC officers in front of a row of land rovers that lined the Garvaghy Road. The land rovers were behind the police, close to the march route; the double line of police officers faced outward toward the protesters. According to Eamon Stack, policemen with plastic bullet guns were placed about every fifth officer in the double lines.

> As the parade turned the corner, the baton charge [against those protesting the march] began. Both lines of officers charged. They were firing at a rate of ten bullets a minute. The crowd is doing nothing! The press was mingling with the crowd. . . I saw an officer point a gun at close range at a crowd standing peacefully. I approached him and asked him why he was doing that as it was extremely dangerous and unnecessary. He just laughed at me. The police line moved parallel to Churchill Park. As the line advanced, the crowd dispersed into alleyways and into the estate.[101]

Protesters in Churchill Park and the surrounding area allege that the RUC fired plastic bullets indiscriminately and many officers hurled sectarian abuse at the protesters as they fired. Martin Beattie told Human Rights Watch/Helsinki that he was holding his child in his arms when he was hit in the back with a plastic bullet.[102] Donna O'Hara reported that she was "as close to the RUC as you are now to me"—approximately three feet—when they began firing plastic bullets:

> Then when they got us into Churchill Park, they opened up with plastic bullets. I saw the RUC start shooting. There were plastic

---

[100]Human Rights Watch/Helsinki visited Churchill Park in November 1996.

[101]Human Rights Watch/Helsinki interview, Portadown, November 17, 1996.

[102]Human Rights Watch/Helsinki interview, Portadown, November 17, 1996.

bullets everywhere. People were hit with these in broad daylight. They called us "Fenian scum," "Fenian bastards." They enjoyed it. I could see the hatred. We ran. We had to hide beneath cars and whatnot.[103]

Sister Laura Boyle told Human Rights Watch/Helsinki that she "saw plastic bullets flying in all directions."[104] Many residents described the scene as police shooting plastic bullets on a peaceful crowd. Some residents who were hit by plastic bullets were not involved in the protests at all:

Gerald Mario Donnelly: I decided to head into Churchill Park to see if any of my sons were out in the trouble. As I was heading across the road, I felt a sharp pain going up my right arm. I fell on one knee, but I got straight up and kept running into Churchill Park. It was at that stage I realized I was hit by a baton round. I was in so much pain, I decided to head back for home.

Jeanette Livingstone: Running into the 12th morning, I was going around to my friend's house who was babysitting for me. As I turned around and passed the alleyways, the next thing I knew I was on the ground and people came and lifted me up and brought me around to my friend's house. I was hit by a plastic bullet on the knee. I didn't see the officer who shot it. I was told by people not to go near the hospital because the police would lift [arrest] anyone who was hit by plastic bullets.

Donna Griffin: Women were screaming, plastic bullets were being fired and I got separated from my son. The RUC shot at nothing. They seemed to get a target and fire.

Eileen McNally: I tried to get to my car but as I reached it a long line of police which had formed started firing plastic bullets. There were thirty or more officers. It was continuous. They seemed to be standing relaxed. I crouched for safety

---

[103]Human Rights Watch/Helsinki interview, Portadown, November 17, 1996.

[104]Human Rights Watch/Helsinki interview, Portadown, November 17, 1996.

behind another car. I could see people running for safety towards the Ashgrove Shopping Centre so I ran with them. Many people were shouting and crying. I could hear many plastic bullets being shot. The police were two widths of the Garvaghy Road away. Their guns were at shoulder height. When the situation began to calm, I ran to my car where I discovered the rear window smashed by a plastic bullet.

Bernadette McGeown: The police were firing plastic bullets at no end. I saw officers shooting at people. They were hit face high.

RUC Chief Constable Ronnie Flanagan told Human Rights Watch/Helsinki that plastic bullets are used "to keep petrol bombers back and to keep cover from gunmen."[105] According to Professor Herbie Wallace, a member of the Police Authority, "Plastic bullets are the most effective and least dangerous way to control crowd violence here. The problem is the widespread use of petrol bombs."[106] RUC guidelines for plastic bullet use require the gunner to target a specific individual from at least twenty meters away and aim below the waist.[107] The police have presented no evidence that the crowd in Churchill Park was exhibiting violent behavior or that petrol bombs threatened either life or property at Churchill Park when the RUC began shooting. The Committee on the Administration of Justice noted that police on the Garvaghy Road "were at no obvious risk" when they started firing.[108] Testimony taken from protesters and residents indicates that the police were not, in fact, responding to any danger. Some residents who were shot were not involved in the protests, some were shot in the back, and many were shot at while standing peacefully in Churchill Park. Indeed, the random and indiscriminate nature of the shooting resulted in damage to parked cars.

---

[105]Human Rights Watch/Helsinki interview, Belfast, November 11, 1996.

[106]Human Rights Watch/Helsinki interview, Belfast, November 11, 1996.

[107]Human Rights Watch/Helsinki interview with RUC Chief Constable Ronnie Flanagan, November 11, 1996.

[108]Committee on the Administration of Justice, *The Misrule of Law*, p. 36.

After the protesters were cleared from the Garvaghy Road, corralled into Churchill Park, and then fired upon with plastic bullets, the Orange Order march proceeded down the Garvaghy Road unconfronted by any protest activity or counter-demonstration. Most of the residents were scattered about the Churchill Park housing estate, fearful of returning to the road after the baton charge.

In the aftermath of Drumcree, Pat Armstrong, the chairperson of the Police Authority, argued that while serious damage was done to the reputation of the RUC, the chief constable and the police force were "being cast as scapegoats:"

> The policing of the recent disorder following the stand-off at Drumcree has called into question the integrity and impartiality of the RUC. It has also raised doubts about the ability of Government to protect the community as a whole, through the maintenance of law and order. As a result, there have been claims from all sides that the RUC's standing has never been lower in recent years. Let there be no mistake, the RUC did not create the situation. The responsibility for the disorder, violence and wanton destruction, which erupted at different times across the province and from both communities falls squarely on the shoulders of those who organised parades and those who sought unlawfully to avert them. Responsibility also lies with those political and community leaders who whipped up sectarian emotions and orchestrated or failed to contain law-breaking and violence.[109]

Human Rights Watch/Helsinki cannot subscribe to this incomplete formulation for calculating blame for the events at Drumcree. Both the government of the United Kingdom and the RUC must be held accountable for their respective roles in these events. Sir Patrick Mayhew cannot escape responsibility by simply stating that he did not influence the police decision. Indeed, if the situation was as tense as the RUC asserted, the government either knew or ought to have known that this was the case, particularly in light of the government's claim that it was in close contact with and fully briefed by Chief Constable Hugh Annesley. The government is thus responsible for the decision to reverse the initial determination to reroute the march whether or not it participated in or formally approved it. The reversal at

---

[109]Police Authority for Northern Ireland, press release, July 1996. The release contained an article by Pat Armstrong which appeared in the *Belfast Telegraph* on July 24, 1996.

Drumcree was clear evidence that the RUC was not up to the task conferred upon it by the government. Police indiscretion and bad judgment merely fueled the mob tactics of the Drumcree unionist protesters. Under the public order legislation in force in Northern Ireland, it would have been appropriate for the government to intervene to stabilize a situation that had degenerated over time into mob rule. Furthermore, the RUC's failure to intervene to halt the violent and illegal acts of the marchers and their supporters, coupled with police officers' response to the protesters on the Garvaghy Road, raise profound questions about the force's impartiality and professionalism. The evidence reviewed by Human Rights Watch/Helsinki indicates that the police response to the Garvaghy Road protesters was characterized by police brutality, sectarian abuse, and the indiscriminate use of plastic bullets resulting in widespread violations of the residents' human rights. Residents who had sought RUC protection from sectarian violence at the hands of Orange Order marchers were ultimately brutalized by the RUC itself.

Events at London/Derry: July 11 to 14, 1996

The reversal at Drumcree and the treatment of protesters on the Garvaghy Road spawned nationalist protests across Northern Ireland. In London/Derry, the nationalist Bogside Residents Group called for a protest march to commence at 7:00 p.m. on July 11, 1996. An estimated 5,000 people turned out and the march proceeded without incident. Some time shortly after midnight on July 12, 1996, the city erupted in violence which left one man dead, hundreds of persons injured, and massive property damage. The accounts of when the violence started, at what time and under what circumstances vary. What remains clear is that many people who were not involved in rioting and who did not pose any threat to life or property were shot with plastic bullets and suffered serious injuries. One man was killed when he was run over by a British army armored personnel carrier. There is also strong evidence to suggest that RUC officers intimidated people trying to gain access to treatment at a local hospital resulting in the drawing and use of batons in an emergency room.

The RUC maintains that the first plastic baton rounds were fired at approximately 1:00 a.m. on July 12, 1996, on Butcher Street:

> A crowd of about 100 persons attacked commercial premises in the area and then threw a barrage of petrol bombs and other missiles at Police. Police responded by firing 6 plastic baton rounds at identified petrol bombers. Extensive damage was

caused to the Heritage Center, a building site and other commercial premises by the petrol bombs.[110]

It is undisputed that serious riots took place in London/Derry on the nights of July 11, 12, and 13, 1996. In April 1997, Human Rights Watch/Helsinki requested information from the RUC about petrol bomb use at London/Derry from July 11 to 14, 1996. We were told that since the summer of 1996, the RUC had revised its methodology with respect to quantifying petrol bomb use and now considered not the total number of petrol bombs thrown but the number of incidents during which petrol bombs were used. Subsequently, we were sent a letter informing us that an estimated 4,000 petrol bombs were thrown.[111]

It is unclear why the RUC decided to provide us with this information instead of the number of incidents of petrol bomb use, but this reversal might reflect the same confusion over gathering and accurately analyzing statistical information that appeared to characterize the summer 1996 marching season. For example, some petrol bomb statistics varied dramatically from day to day and were revised several times in July and August 1996 according to a number of official sources. One police federation official estimated that petrol bombs "probably in excess of 20,000" were thrown by nationalists.[112] The RUC reported a total number of petrol bombs thrown at anywhere from 800 to over 4,000.[113] A different problem applied to the calculation of plastic bullets fired. The RUC initially estimated that 6,002 plastic bullets were fired from July 7 to 14, 1996, in the whole of Northern Ireland.[114] The revised figure as of March 1997 was a total of 6,921

---

[110]Letter from RUC Chief Constable Ronnie Flanagan to Human Rights Watch/Helsinki, Table 7, March 7, 1997.

[111]Letter to Human Rights Watch/Helsinki from RUC Chief Superintendent G.W. Sillery, May 12, 1997.

[112]Brendan Anderson, "RUC Union Magazine Defends Force Actions," *Irish News*, August 9, 1996.

[113]Committee on the Administration of Justice, *Misrule of Law*, p. 34.

[114]Letter from RUC Chief Constable Ronnie Flanagan to Human Rights Watch/Helsinki, Table 5, March 7, 1997.

plastic bullets fired by police and army over that week.[115]   The RUC attributed this variation to an extensive analysis and validation of disaggregated information received following the summer's events.[116]   The latest revision in the number of plastic bullets fired accounts for 900 rounds that were not included in the earlier statistics. While Human Rights Watch/Helsinki appreciates that keeping statistics in situations of public disorder can be difficult, the use of numbers to justify the RUC's claims that it was embattled—and thus had a legitimate reason to respond with great force—requires a more careful and immediate analysis than that performed in the summer of 1996.[117]   The variation in statistics and changes in methodology *post fact* appears to point to either sloppy inventory and recording practices or to a deliberate attempt to deflate or inflate numbers in order to justify RUC actions.

Problems with keeping track of the number of plastic bullets fired also may have been a result of the indiscriminate shooting of a massive number of plastic baton rounds. Testimony taken by Human Rights Watch/Helsinki indicates that plastic bullets were fired indiscriminately at London/Derry in situations where the police were not in any danger. People were shot in the back, shot as they rounded corners, and targeted despite reports that no rioting was occurring around them. The indiscriminate use of plastic bullets led to the escalation of violence by causing unnecessary and often severe injuries, and by contributing to a general climate of tension, fear and confusion.

Human Rights Watch/Helsinki interviewed many people who testified that they were not rioting nor was rioting going on around them when they were hit with plastic bullets. Michael McEleney told us that he was going to pick up his sister, at his mother's request, on the night of July 11 to 12, when he was struck in the face with a plastic bullet. He believes the shot came from the top of a parking garage:

> I walked up to go to Henry J.'s [pub]. I heard bullet shots and I
> put my head around the corner. There was nothing happening
> down the street. The RUC were at Castle Gate, on the top and

---

[115]Ibid.

[116]Ibid.

[117]The "problem" of statistics appears several times in this report. Where appropriate, we note how we arrived at our statistics and why the numbers reflected in other reports of the events of summer 1996 do not conform to our own.

jeeps were parked at the archways. I was hit at Waterloo and Castle. Two guys carried me away. I knew it was bad because I was losing a lot of blood. There was constant shooting. I had to keep bowing my head because of the shooting. No taxis would take me over to Altnagelvin [Hospital]. The taxis were afraid to go to the hospital. I finally got a taxi but it left me off outside the hospital. As I was coming into the hospital, I saw the police and the Brits. They were standing with dogs at the doorway and they laughed at me. I don't know what they found so funny. I had a discomnected jaw. My jaw, sinus bone and palate were all broken. The bullet went through all the layers of skin. I spent two days in hospital and then had surgery. They stitched it, put wire in the jaw, wired my teeth and I was on a liquid diet. I lost about a stone. There is permanent paralysis in my mouth.[118]

A sample of testimony from other victims includes:[119]

William Noel Nash, age twenty-four: Thursday evening [July 11 to 12] I was in the Strand Bar for a drink about 1:00 a.m. We tried to get out the front door on to the Strand Road. We had to go out the back entrance. We were standing by the gate waiting for the shooting of plastic bullets to die down. Once it died down, we tried to walk through the lane from the bar to Sackville Street. I heard a bang and was hit in the back of the head. They all fired at one time. There were five in my group; one got hit on the leg, one on the kneecap, and one in the stomach. We thought the RUC had gone! I didn't see them; they fired at us from behind. I passed out and was carried to the corner of Russell Street. The guys who were trying to carry me were hit, too. My brother and mom took me to Letterkenny Hospital. I had a fractured skull.

Darren Large, age eighteen: [July 13] People were dropping, lying on the ground, getting carried everywhere. Some RUC

---

[118]Human Rights Watch/Helsinki interview, London/Derry, November 23, 1996.

[119]Human Rights Watch/Helsinki interviews, London/Derry, November 23, 1996.

men were bouncing bullets off the wall so they wouldn't hit people full force. Some were aiming them in the air, straight up so they dropped down on the crowd. I was just standing there watching then I felt this big shot on my leg and I blacked out. I woke up on Russell Street where they were putting people in taxis to help. I was not throwing stones or petrol bombs. I've never been in a riot before.

Martina Hagerty, age twenty-nine: [Early hours of July 13] Both army and RUC were shooting. I saw them. I took an alleyway behind the Pilots Row Community Center. I got to the other side of the street, my back was toward the police. The RUC were a good bit away. The rioting was happening down beside the RUC. Where I was, people were just standing outside watching. I was standing with my back to the whole lot. I got hit in the side of the right foot and had a fractured heel. There wasn't anyone beside me or next to me who was doing anything for them to shoot.

Caoimhghin O'Murchadha, a member of the Bogside Residents Group, also claimed that plastic bullets were shot at people trying to leave bars and clubs on the night of July 11:

Later that night I heard a noise. It was a crowd squealing. There was a trail of refugees, bloody, in "going out" clothes running from the city center. The police were waiting in riot gear at the top of the hill. They blocked off all exits but Shipquay Gate. I saw police shooting plastic bullets into the crowd. At the time, people were leaving the pubs. They were all dressed for going out. It was forty to fifty minutes before the petrol bombs started.[120]

Human Rights Watch/Helsinki heard many allegations that the police were out of control and sought to provoke violence. Martin Finucane, a representative of the Pat Finucane Centre who organized groups of observers over the three nights of violence at London/Derry, described how police appeared to enjoy shooting plastic bullets and fired at will:

---

[120]Human Rights Watch/Helsinki interview, London/Derry, November 23, 1996.

I was behind police lines from about midnight on Thursday evening [July 11] until 6:30 the following morning. There were plenty of stones and rocks being thrown and petrol bombs. And never once did I feel threatened. Most of the objects and bottles were falling short. They [the RUC] used armored vehicles! The RUC were in a jovial mood. If they hit anybody, they said, "Yes!" The photojournalist I was with asked the RUC why they were firing so many plastic bullets. He said, "because they deserve it." Most of the media gathered behind the army and the RUC cordon at Little James Street. I witnessed some soldiers , Scottish Highlanders, being consulted by an officer. They were in riot gear in a huddle. I distinctly heard the officer say, "What do we want? When do we want it? Now!" He was psyching them up. Throughout the time on Little James Street, the RUC and military ran out of plastic bullets three times that evening. The first time they ran out of bullets the order was to fire on petrol bombers only. After that, it was fire at will, hit anything that moves. There was such overuse that three or four plastic bullet guns had overheated and jammed and one officer stated that this had never happened before. On the first occasion, fifteen to twenty boxes [of bullets] were brought from Strand Road. I witnessed an RUC inspector going, "Yes! Yes! Good job boys!" I just felt it was sickening. It was a duck shoot. There were times throughout the night when three to four deep RUC officers were firing, just firing. It was like confetti when you looked at it.[121]

The large number of injuries from plastic bullets coupled with the refusal of many taxi drivers to transport the injured to a nearby hospital resulted in the establishment of casualty units in the homes of some residents in London/Derry. Patricia Sheerin had one of the largest of these "home hospitals" and by July 13, 1996, her house had become the treatment center for the most serious injuries:

A couple of fellows were running with a fellow who'd been hit and laid him on the ground. I went over to see how he was, but the plastic bullets. . . they were just steady firing them. I said

---

[121]Human Rights Watch/Helsinki interview, London/Derry, November 23, 1996.

bring him up to my house. After that, there was a steady stream. A lot on the upper back; they were hit from behind. The house became a casualty unit. There were a lot of leg and back injuries on Thursday night. By Saturday, it was all head injuries. There were well over 200 people in and out. Saturday night a fellow came in. The whole top lip was just hanging off. Six first aiders showed up and I don't know what we would have done without them. The injuries seemed to be getting steadily worse. By Saturday, I was convinced they were out to kill. On Thursday evening, I had people trapped in my house. The RUC made a charge up the road. One of the women then came out to look to see if they'd gone. The RUC man was on the balcony above. When she put her head out, he pointed the gun. They were firing from there. On Thursday, some of the fellas were very young. Most of them were *not* rioting. They were at Squire's or the Strand Bar. You knew by the way they were dressed. They were out for the night. Not for rioting. They were in bars and when they come out, the RUC were firing baton rounds on Shipquay Street. You're talking 600 young ones coming out of these dance halls.

Chief Constable Ronnie Flanagan told Human Rights Watch/Helsinki that RUC intelligence indicated the nationalist community planned the massive violence that erupted at London/Derry on July 11 to 14, 1996.[122] Flanagan said he knew of arrangements that were made for consignments of petrol to London/Derry, and that the violence was "orchestrated." In response to allegations that the RUC provoked the violence, Flanagan stated:

I don't accept that version of events. There were plans made. We knew on specific intelligence what was planned at Derry. I stand with the version of events that say the police reacted to violence as opposed to initiating violence.[123]

---

[122]Human Rights Watch/Helsinki interview, Belfast, November 24, 1996.

[123]Ibid.

Events at Altnagelvin Hospital

Allegations of police provocation extend to events at Altnagelvin Hospital in London/Derry on the night of July 11 to 12, 1996. Several people we interviewed charged the police with intimidating behavior at the entrance to the Altnagelvin casualty unit. Moreover, eyewitnesses accuse the RUC of leading a baton charge inside the unit.

According to the mother of Michael McEleny, when she got to Altnagelvin Hospital:

> The whole entrance was RUC, soldiers, and a couple of dogs. The policemen were laughing and joking, "Oh, there's another one!" I felt intimidated to walk inside the hospital. I felt afraid walking past them. The police were inside the hospital at one point with a dog. There was a woman there who told the police to leave the hospital. The police were provoking the people.[124]

Michaela McEleny, Michael's sister, arrived at Altnagelvin Hospital after hearing that her brother had been seriously injured by a plastic bullet:

> The police were outside the hospital laughing and joking. An RUC woman officer was injured. When she came out of the hospital, she was cheered and they were clapping for her. With all these other people covered in blood, with their ears hanging off them, they were cheering.[125]

The news that the RUC were outside Altnagelvin spread quickly and many of the injured refused to go to the hospital for treatment for fear that the police would arrest them for rioting. According to Patricia Sheerin:

> On Thursday, one of the ambulance drivers told me, "Don't let them go near casualty. They're [the RUC] waiting on them." I had all these people with me and they couldn't even go to hospital. The head injuries wouldn't even go. There were cars in

---

[124]Human Rights Watch/Helsinki interview, London/Derry, November 23, 1996.

[125]Human Rights Watch/Helsinki interview, London/Derry, November 23, 1996.

front of my house taking people to Letterkenny [Hospital]. It would take nearly an hour to get there.[126]

Patrick Friel, twenty-one years old, told Human Rights Watch/Helsinki that he was hit in the head by a plastic bullet as he was coming out of the Oakgrove Bar on Bishop Street and was taken to Altnagelvin Hospital. Friel reported that RUC officers entered the casualty unit with a police dog and became involved in an altercation:

> At the hospital there were all cops outside and inside. I was sitting in the waiting room not far from the door. There was name calling between the cops and ones waiting to get treated. About a dozen or more cops came in with a dog and the dog went for a fella and the cops started belting people with batons. They just went mad.[127]

Testimony taken by the Committee on the Administration of Justice and the Pat Finucane Centre supports the conclusion that RUC officers outside the hospital were engaged in intimidatory behavior and that officers entered the hospital and drew batons on persons waiting for treatment or accompanying someone waiting for treatment in the casualty unit.[128] Moreover, the RUC has confirmed that a number of complaints were lodged against police officers in relation to the incident at Altnagelvin.[129]

---

[126]Human Rights Watch/Helsinki interview, London/Derry, November 23, 1996. Letterkenny Hospital is approximately twenty miles from London/Derry across the border in County Donegal, the Republic of Ireland. Ms. Sheerin noted that it would take an hour because people would be forced to take back roads to avoid the RUC.

[127]Human Rights Watch/Helsinki interview, London/Derry, November 23, 1996. Patrick Friel suffered a compound fracture and an "abrasion to the brain" from the plastic bullet shot. He was transferred to the Royal Victoria Hospital in Belfast after developing a clot on his brain and spent six days in the hospital. Friel told Human Rights Watch/Helsinki there was no rioting going on when he left the bar and got hit.

[128]See Committee on the Administration of Justice, *The Misrule of Law*, pp. 44-47; Appendix III, pp. 95.; and Pat Finucane Centre, *In the Line of Fire*, pp. 20-21.

[129]Letter from RUC Chief Superintendent G. W. Sillery to the Committee on the Administration of Justice, RUC Ref: Com Sec 96/261/10, March 28, 1997.

Stella Burnside, chief executive at Altnagelvin, told Human Rights Watch/Helsinki that an internal investigation focusing on impediments to access to treatment had been conducted in the immediate aftermath of the incident. The investigation addressed two issues: 1) the safety of hospital staff and their freedom to care freely for people; and 2) the right of all persons to have access to treatment regardless of who they are or what activities they have been engaged in. Although the results of the investigation have not been made public, Ms. Burnside reported that the inquiry has resulted in the implementation of new procedures in order to guarantee unimpeded access to medical care at Altnagelvin: 1) realigned entry and security systems to assure that the hospital can cordon off areas in which an altercation occurs; 2) clear protocols which allow a person who is under threat from another person—when both are being treated at the same time—to be treated in separate spaces. Ms. Burnside claimed that the July 1996 events were not the sole reason for the internal investigation but served to speed up an assessment that was on-going.[130]

In many instances, it is common police procedure to check hospitals for perpetrators of crimes. However, the RUC's conduct at the hospital—laughing at the injured, clapping for an RUC officer in the midst of numerous injured people and using a police dog at the entrance—was, at best, insensitive and at worst, served to exacerbate tensions in an extremely charged situation. This behavior is in stark contrast to what might reasonably be expected of law enforcement officials at such a difficult time, that is, a basic duty to *defuse* tensions wherever possible. Furthermore, the presence of RUC officers at the entrance to the hospital on the night of July 11 to 12, gave rise to fears over the next two days that the police were attempting to justify the shooting of large numbers of plastic bullets by seeking out persons injured by plastic baton rounds at the hospital in order to charge them with rioting.

The Death of Dermot McShane

Dermot McShane, a thirty-five year old man, died after being run over by a British army armored personnel carrier on the night of July 12 to 13, 1996, in London/Derry. By all accounts, the rioting in the city was intense that night. According to several eyewitnesses, RUC land rovers and army vehicles filled the

---

[130]Human Rights Watch/Helsinki telephone interview, April 25, 1997. Stella Burnside denies press accounts which claim that she asked the RUC to leave the hospital in the early morning hours of July 12. Ms. Burnside told Human Rights Watch/Helsinki that when she arrived on the scene, the police were already beginning to leave the hospital. Ibid.

streets. Oistín MacBride, a photojournalist, reported that the city center was in chaos:

> I moved..towards the corner of Little James Street where
> approximately 20 RUC personnel were standing in full riot gear.
> As I moved in that direction, a contingent of British soldiers
> arrived in jeeps and a number of Saxon armored personnel
> carriers.[131] They all moved to Little James Street adjacent to the
> Post Office. [The soldiers and RUC] formed a cordon with the
> majority of soldiers to the left as you face the Bogside and RUC
> to the right. There was an intense barrage of missiles being fired
> towards the cordon and plastic bullets were being fired at will by
> both soldiers and RUC.   There was considerable confusion
> between RUC and soldiers about what they were doing...The
> RUC man in charge was receiving radio messages about what to
> do and he cursed violently several times to another officer
> saying, "These fucking cunts can't make up their mind...we're
> not going in now."[132]

Dermot McShane was standing in the middle of Little James Street behind a hoarding (a large piece of board) which was held up by him and a number of other people. It remains unclear whether the people using the hoarding were shielding themselves from a hail of plastic bullets in an attempt to get across the street or whether they were using it as cover from behind which they were throwing petrol bombs at the security forces.[133]   In either event, a British army Saxon veered away from a cordon of vehicles, hit the hoarding and ran over it, crushing Dermot McShane who, later that night, died from his injuries.

Despite the disorder, witnesses in Little James Street that night claim that it was obvious there were people holding up the hoarding. Martin Finucane witnessed the advance of security force vehicles upon the rioting crowd that led to the death of Dermot McShane:

---

[131]Saxon is a brand name for armored personnel carriers used by the British army.

[132]Written statement by Oistin MacBride to the Pat Finucane Centre re: Events of 13 July 1996. Human Rights Watch/Helsinki confirmed the contents of this statement with Oistin MacBride in a telephone interview on April 24, 1997.

[133]Committee on the Administration of Justice, *The Misrule of Law*, p. 43.

Rioters were hiding behind a refuse bin and a number of people were behind a hoarding. There was one officer with a hand held speaker and a sergeant giving orders, too. They were giving their orders to move forward and at the same time to fire in volleys and to "hit anything that moves." They moved forward slowly. I was standing about twelve to fifteen feet behind the cordon [of vehicles]. One of the army Saxons moved away from the line of the cordon and toward the hoarding. The street lights were on, there was clear visibility. A hoarding doesn't stand up on its own. It was visible that people were behind the hoarding. As they advanced, the crowd diffused. The vehicle pursued and hit the hoarding. The vehicle stopped momentarily after it hit the hoarding and then moved forward slowly. The people behind the hoarding didn't get away. I saw one man cradling another in his arms and saying, "This man's seriously injured and he needs help! Please help me!" At that stage the media moved in. Oistin said, "Martin, go grab him!" Then two RUC officers grabbed Dermot McShane around the collar and shoulders and began to drag him away from the scene. It was myself who reached down and grabbed Dermot McShane by his left leg. We lifted him and took him back to the side of the post office and the RUC began first aid.[134]

It was also reported that an RUC officer was attacked and slashed in the face with a broken bottle while he attempted to administer first aid to Dermot McShane, requiring nineteen stitches to his face.[135]

The week after Dermot McShane's death, RUC Chief Constable Hugh Annesley appointed a senior RUC detective to lead an investigation of the incident.[136] Treasa McShane, Dermot McShane's wife, told Human Rights Watch/Helsinki that the investigation was riddled with problems. Mrs. McShane was not contacted by the RUC until July 30, 1996, and was not interviewed until

---

[134]Human Rights Watch/Helsinki interview, London/Derry, November 23, 1996.

[135]See Darwin Templeton and George Jackson, "Riot Death Fuels Nationalist Fury," *Sunday Life*, July 14, 1996; Paul Routledge, et. al., "Ulster Peace Talks on Brink of Collapse," *The Independent*, July 14, 1996.

[136]Pat Finucane Center, *In the Line of Fire*, p. 22.

October 2.[137] In the meantime, Mrs. McShane obtained legal counsel and brought a civil action against the United Kingdom Ministry of Defense for criminally negligent use of a vehicle.

According to Jane Corr, Treasa McShane's lawyer, Corr was assured by a police detective on August 13, 1996, that the RUC was taking the McShane investigation "very seriously." Corr asked the detective if the driver of the Saxon that ran over Dermot McShane had been interviewed by the RUC. The detective told her that he had not. It was not until the October 2 meeting of Treasa McShane and Jane Corr with the RUC that they were informed that the driver had been interviewed on August 29, 1996— seven weeks after the incident occurred.[138]

The RUC told Jane Corr in October 1996 that the investigation into Dermot McShane's death would take six to eight weeks because there was "difficulty in taking statements."[139] It is correct that one eyewitness refused to cooperate with the RUC despite a public plea by the force for this witness to come forward.[140] Oistin MacBride, however, witnessed the event and administered aid to Dermot McShane in the immediate aftermath of the Saxon's advance over the hoarding, but was never contacted or interviewed by the RUC. According to MacBride, he is well-known to the RUC, he and Martin Finucane were the closest civilian witnesses to the incident, and he was willing to cooperate with the investigation.[141]

Jane Corr reports that, as of April 25, 1997, the RUC have not contacted her directly since October 1996. As far as she knows, the status of the investigation remains the same as it was in November 1996 when Human Rights Watch/Helsinki first spoke with her, and no inquest has been scheduled.[142]

---

[137]Human Rights Watch/Helsinki interview, London/Derry, November 7, 1996.

[138]Human Rights Watch/Helsinki interview, London/Derry, November 7, 1996. The RUC confirmed that it had finally interviewed the driver of the saxon in a letter dated September 3, 1996, to Jane Corr.

[139]Ibid.

[140]Human Rights Watch/Helsinki telephone interview with the witness, May 6, 1997.

[141]Human Rights Watch/Helsinki telephone interview, April 24, 1997.

[142]Human Rights Watch/Helsinki telephone interview, April 25, 1997.

Events on the Lower Ormeau Road, Belfast: July 11 to 12, 1996

The Orange Order planned to march down the Lower Ormeau Road in south Belfast on the morning of July 12, 1996. The Lower Ormeau Concerned Community (LOCC), a nationalist residents' group, sought an injunction on July 11, 1996, in the Belfast High Court to prohibit the march from proceeding. The court did not grant the injunction. Despite the denial of the injunction, it was still within the discretion of the RUC to order the march rerouted. By 6:00 p.m. that evening, however, the predominantly nationalist Lower Ormeau community was saturated with police and army vehicles and personnel. A near total curfew was imposed for at least seventeen hours with movement into and out of the community severely restricted. The RUC never officially informed the residents that the march would be permitted, but the heavy police presence—focused as it was on containing the nationalist community—was an obvious indication that the Orange Order would be allowed to proceed. The march commenced the next morning at approximately 9:00 a.m.

Father Peter McCann, a priest at St. Malachy's whose parish includes the Lower Ormeau Road, described the police operation and its effect on the community to Human Rights Watch/Helsinki:

> Land rovers were blocking doorways. I went to one house where a land rover was parked in front of the door and asked that the land rover be removed. The driver refused and said, "see the officer in charge." Only residents of the Lower Ormeau Road were not allowed on the road. Others came and went freely. People couldn't get into their homes if they weren't on a register. People were locked in by the river on one side and a solid row of land rovers on the other. There was no notice. People couldn't go to shops, for medical care or whatever. If you were a resident of the area, you had no freedom to move.[143]

Martin Morgan, a Social Democratic and Labour Party (SDLP) councillor, stated that he arrived on the Lower Ormeau Road at approximately 8:00 p.m.:

> There were large numbers of RUC along the Ormeau Road...As well as this, large numbers of RUC/soldiers were placed in

---

[143]Human Rights Watch/Helsinki interview, Belfast, November 9, 1996. The "others" Father McCann refers to included a cadre of both local and international press and television reporters and contingents of parliamentary and nongovernmental observers.

arterial streets along the entire length and on both sides of the Ormeau Road...I witnessed RUC land rovers blockading each street on the Nationalist side of the Ormeau Road...The RUC were behaving in an intimidatory manner towards the people and were clearly disrupting the ordinary, everyday lives of the people by putting such a massive cordon in place, the positioning of the land rovers at each street and by the attitudes of the security forces towards local residents.[144]

Margaret O'Kane, age fifty-four, told Human Rights Watch/Helsinki that there was a blanket of RUC in the area when she tried to return to her home between 6:00 and 6:30 p.m. Mrs. O'Kane was not allowed access to her home because she could not show identification:

I asked a police officer, "Can I get in?" and he said, "No, if you don't have identification" which I didn't have. So, I went to my daughter's house and phoned Donegal Pass, the police station, and asked to speak to whoever was in charge. I asked the duty officer for his name and he refused. He told me I wasn't allowed into my home. He said, "Look, speak to the people down on the ground or else come in and make an official complaint." I told him if I could get to him, I could get into my own home! I slept at my daughter's house.[145]

The RUC appeared to make no exceptions with respect to the movement of Lower Ormeau residents. Tony Shields was driving to collect his daughter when he was stopped by the RUC in the early evening of July 11:

I was going down Farnham Street and was stopped by the police. They asked where I was going and I told them number thirty-nine. They said, "You're not going anywhere. Leave your car in the road." I just drove on. The police stopped me and dragged me out of the car. I had my seatbelt on. Then they started kicking me in the chest and all over my body. They threw me in

---

[144]Statement from Martin Morgan to Madden & Finucane Solicitors, dated July 31, 1996.

[145]Human Rights Watch/Helsinki interview, Belfast, November 9, 1996.

the back of a truck and beat me with batons. "We'll fix you!"
they said. They gave no reason but it was obvious it was because
I was defying them. I was all bruised and sore. They took me to
the station and threw me in a cell.[146]

Ann McCartan witnessed this assault:

I came out the door of my house and saw ten officers lifting up
Tony Shields' car and one of the officers was beating him with
a baton inside the jeep. Everyone was squealing and shouting.
One of the RUC officers placed his hands on my shoulders and
pushed me back into my house. But I saw that another jeep was
sent for and backed right up to the other jeep and they opened
the doors and Tony got out. The side of his face was all bloody.
I saw him again at his house on Farnham at about 12:30 -1:00
a.m.. He was all marked and there were footprints on his t-shirt
and trousers.[147]

While some residents were not allowed into the area for any reason, other
residents were not allowed out of their own homes for any reason. The following
testimonies indicate that the RUC was not prepared to allow people to leave for
medical emergencies, to care for elderly or infirm relatives or to obtain food:[148]

Meg McReynolds: My father just had a tumor removed. He's
got very bad cancer and part of his stomach is also gone. He
lives at the top of the corner. I asked the RUC officer, "Could
I please go in and see my father? He's had a major operation and
I need to attend him." He told me to "fuck off!" I even offered
to have the police accompany me and he said "fuck off!" again.
My father lives above the bakery and has no phone. He has no
neighbors I could call to ask to check on him. I saw him at 4:30
- 5:00 p.m. [on July 11] when I took him his dinner. At 1:00
a.m., he got to a window and I shouted up to him did he need

[146]Human Rights Watch/Helsinki interview, Belfast, November 9, 1996.

[147]Human Rights Watch/Helsinki interview, Belfast, November 9, 1996.

[148]Human Rights Watch/Helsinki interviews, Belfast, November 9, 1996.

anything? I finally got to him after 4:00 p.m. the next day. He was very distracted. He had managed to eat something on his own.

Ann McCartan, mother of a seven-year-old boy: My wee boy has asthma and they wouldn't let me get a taxi and take him to hospital. He had an attack and I went up to the officer and said "My son has asthma and can't breathe." He told me, "Just get back into your fucking house." I couldn't get out. I phoned the doctor and he couldn't get in. He told me to steam the whole bathroom. My son was bad the whole night. It's the worst I'd actually seen him. By the morning, he was starting to breathe again.

Charlie Fisher: At about 5:00 a.m. on July 12, a land rover blocked off the door to the building. I live above the post office and only have one entrance. The back windows are covered with grills.

Sean Beckett: I live on the Ormeau Road, Number 162. On July 12, 1996, there were three of us in the flat. A land rover parked right in front of the door, about three inches away. We were in bed. It was 5:30 a.m. We jumped out of bed. We were blocked in. I asked the RUC, "What happens if a fire starts here?" He said, "It's your fuckin' tough luck" and sang "Let the River Run Free." I told the RUC I was going to the shop to get milk for the child. I climbed over the land rover and was grabbed by the driver. He let me go for milk and return the same way.

Sean Beckett also reported that his mother-in law was claustrophobic and asthmatic and needed an inhaler but the RUC would not let him out of his house to get it. A television reporter threw an inhaler up to him from the street.[149]

Government representatives and the RUC told Human Rights Watch/Helsinki that the restrictions imposed on residents of the Lower Ormeau Road were preventive measures meant to protect the community from harm. According to John Steele, a Northern Ireland Office official, the common law "duty of care" underpins the British tradition of policing which gives the police

---

[149]Ibid.

broad powers to maintain the peace.[150] Steele maintained that the RUC could impose restrictions such as those measures taken on the Lower Ormeau Road without consultation with the government as a function of the force's duty to protect the community.[151] RUC Chief Constable Ronnie Flanagan stated that there was great fear that a Drumcree-type situation would be repeated on the Lower Ormeau Road and that, upon reliable police intelligence, violence was imminent if the Orange Order were not allowed to march:

> Don't let me understate the objectionable nature of such a heavy presence in such a small area, but there was a risk of this degenerating into a civil war. We had an absolute duty to preserve the peace. Why on earth would we do this knowing the damage that would be done to our reputation as an impartial police force? It was done *for* that community.[152]

These claims raise troubling questions about the extent of the police operation on the Lower Ormeau Road. Testimony taken by Human Rights Watch/Helsinki indicates that the near curfew-like conditions imposed by the RUC continued into the evening of July 12. Ostensibly the police remained to protect the residents from Orangemen who would be returning from the march through the area. The justification for the continued police presence focused on fears that marchers might cause a disturbance as they returned along a nearby river embankment and over the Ormeau Bridge, or that the residents themselves might attack returning marchers. However, numerous residents reported acts of intimidation, violence, and sectarian abuse by the very police officers allegedly invested with the responsibility to protect them:[153]

> **Isabel Collins:** On July 12 the police were still here. We walked up and saw two police officers in a footpath. There were two wee boys, nine or ten years old, one of them was my nephew. One of the RUC officers told my nephew's friend,

---

[150]Human Rights Watch/Helsinki interview, Belfast, November 11, 1996.

[151]Ibid.

[152]Human Rights Watch/Helsinki interview, Belfast, November 11, 1996.

[153]Human Rights Watch/Helsinki interviews, Belfast, November 9, 1996.

"You can't go to your house." I said to the female RUC officer, "Why can he not go home? A child of ten, is he going to shoot you or blow you up?" I told the child to go home but the officer said, "It'll take just a minute. Just wait. I must check him out."

At about 12:30 p.m. a group of seventeen and eighteen-year-olds took a van and started it on fire at the end of the street. As I made my way up Shaftsbury to tell the mother of the van owner, there was a land rover came flying down the Ormeau Road. There were people sitting and drinking on a wall and the land rover flew straight at the people on the wall. Everyone jumped off the wall but for one man. He jumped off but the land rover pinned him against the wall. The poor fella couldn't move. Officers in the land rover got out and more jeeps came down. They were in riot gear. There must've been forty of them in that corner. I saw the fella drop to the ground and about five officers went over and were hitting him with batons. There was a family standing in the path and the police told them to go inside and when they refused they started beating them. I shouted at a guy with a camera, "Where's the cameras now!" and he came right over and took some shots. One of the police officers called him over and took the camera and pulled the film out.

Margaret O'Kane: I came home at lunch time on July 12. I came into Rugby Avenue and told the officer there that I wanted into my house and that my daughter needed her insulin. The RUC officer said, "You can go, but your daughter can't." She couldn't go because she wasn't a resident. I had to go down and get her injections and bring them back up the road! The bands were well past and our place was still curfewed.

Ann McCartan: On July 12, after the march, I was standing at the gate in front of my house. There were two jeeps full of them [RUC officers]. They were yelling at me, "Get into your fucking house, whore!" One of them was pretending to jerk himself off and he yelled, "Suck my fucking cock!" I didn't respond. I was gobsmacked. There were two of them across the street. They lifted two crates of empty milk bottles and threw them at me. Another one threw an additional crate. The bottles landed

outside on the road. My seven year old came down and started
crying as the third crate was being thrown. He wet the bed for
two weeks after. Normally, he doesn't wet the bed.

Sean Beckett's wife asked the RUC to remove the jeep from in front of her
door after the march had passed. The officer in front of her house told the driver
to "Move it for the fucking bitch" and the land rover was moved.[154]

It remains unclear how the RUC, having asserted that it was stretched to
its limits at Drumcree, could marshall the forces necessary to impose a near total
curfew on an entire community the very next day. As Michael Lavery, chairman
of the Standing Advisory Commission for Human Rights, told Human Rights
Watch/Helsinki, "The previous day, the RUC had no resources to hold back a
howling band of Orangemen but the next day it could imprison an entire
community."[155]

Plastic Bullets

The most controversial weapon used by the police in Northern Ireland for
crowd control is the plastic bullet, technically referred to as the plastic baton round.
The RUC claims that the bullets create space between officers and rioters and cause
fewer and less severe injuries than live ammunition.[156] Despite the claim that the
weapon limits casualties, fourteen people, seven of them children, have been killed
in Northern Ireland by plastic bullets between 1974 and 1996, and there have been
hundreds of injuries.[157] The number of injuries has been augmented significantly
by the hundreds of injuries inflicted by plastic baton rounds fired during the violent
events of the summer of 1996.[158] That plastic bullets are considered non-lethal

---

[154]Ibid.

[155]Human Rights Watch/Helsinki interview, Belfast, November 8, 1996.

[156]Helsinki Watch interview with RUC Chief Constable Hugh Annesley, Belfast,
January 1991. See Helsinki Watch, *Human Rights in Northern Ireland*, p. 63.

[157]Ibid., Appendix D, pp. 159-161, for a complete list of persons killed by plastic
bullets.

[158]An exact number of injuries is difficult to determine. Reporting of plastic bullet
injuries is low because those who go to the hospital or might lodge official complaints have
grounds for fearing that they will be charged with rioting whether or not they were involved

alternatives, their sometimes lethal effects not comparable to the carnage resulting from the use of conventional munitions, has led to a readiness on the part of the RUC to resort to their promiscuous use in a manner that would be unthinkable were they authorized to employ live ammunition.

Plastic bullets were introduced to replace rubber bullets (which killed three people in 1972 and 1973). The plastic bullet is 3½ inches long and 1½ inches in diameter and its ends are flat. Its weight is 4.75 ounces, comparable to that of a cricket ball. The bullet leaves the barrel of a gun at over 160 miles per hour.[159] From 1973 through 1996, 64,200 plastic bullets were reportedly fired in Northern Ireland.[160] The peak year was 1981 when 29,695 bullets were reportedly fired

---

in the violence. In January 1997, Gregory Campbell, security spokesperson for the Democratic Unionist Party (DUP), raised the concern of under reporting in a question to Dr. Maurice Hayes, a government-appointed expert tasked with reviewing the police complaints system:

> First of all, a person makes a complaint concerning alleged action by a police officer. Initially, the complainant does not have charges leveled against him, but subsequently he is charged by police. How do you see a scenario in which such problems could arise, as will undoubtedly be the case if the public order situation we had last summer [1996] occurs next summer [1997]?

Dr. Hayes responded that he had spoken to many solicitors who routinely advise their clients not to make a complaint because it would put them at risk. Hayes felt that his recommendation of a police ombudsman for Northern Ireland "could help." Northern Ireland Forum for Political Dialogue, "Record of Debates," No. 25, January 24, 1997, p. 12. (See also chapter on "Policing in Northern Ireland" for discussion of police ombudsman). Many people who gave testimony to Human Rights Watch/Helsinki, especially people we interviewed in London/Derry about the events of July 11 to 14, 1996, confirmed that they would not report their plastic bullet injuries for fear of prosecution for rioting.

[159]Committee on the Administration of Justice, *Plastic Bullets and the Law* (Belfast: CAJ, March 1990), p. 1.

[160]From 1973-1980, 13,004 plastic bullets were reported fired. See United Campaign Against Plastic Bullets, *A Report on the Misuse of the Baton Round in the North of Ireland: Submission to the Mitchell Commission on Arms Decommissioning,* January 18, 1996, p. 6; From 1981-1984, 32,613 plastic bullets were reported fired. See Committee on the Administration of Justice, *The Misrule of Law,* Appendix I, p. 77 (citing statistics provided by the Irish Information Partnership); from 1985-1996, 18,583 plastic bullets were reported fired. Letter from RUC Chief Constable Ronnie Flanagan to Human Rights Watch/Helsinki, Table 4, March 7, 1997.

during the hunger strikes.[161]   Significantly, the second highest officially acknowledged number of plastic bullets fired in a given year was 7,294 in 1996.[162] The RUC reported 6,721 plastic bullets fired by police and 200 fired by the British army from July 7 to 14, 1996. In London/Derry alone, 2,815 plastic bullets were fired by the police and army from July 11 to 14, 1996.[163]

Opposition groups claim that plastic bullets can be lethal. They also charge the RUC with misuse of the weapon by failing to follow the force's internal guidelines for plastic baton round firing. One week prior to the stand-off at Drumcree, and in recognition of the rising tensions surrounding the marching season, a coalition of human rights and civil liberties groups wrote to Hugh Annesley, then RUC chief constable, urging him "to immediately and permanently withdraw plastic bullets from use."[164] On July 11, 1996, the RUC responded by stating:

> Plastic baton rounds are an essential element of police operational equipment for dealing with serious public disorder, and are only used during periods of serious public disorder. They are used in accord with the principle of the minimum and reasonable amount of force necessary for the protection of life

---

[161]Committee on the Administration of Justice, *The Misrule of Law*, Appendix I, p. 77.

[162]Letter from RUC Chief Constable Ronnie Flanagan to Human Rights Watch/Helsinki, Table 4, March 7, 1997.

[163]Ibid. Original statistics for the number of plastic bullets fired at London/Derry were issued in August 1996 at 3,006 and were later amended in October 1996 to 3,026. See Committee on the Administration of Justice, *Misrule of Law*, p. 27. Human Rights Watch/Helsinki's number of 2,815 is the most recent statistic but according to the RUC, "the figure may be subject to minor adjustment." Letter from Ronnie Flanagan, Table 6, March 7, 1997.

[164]Letter to Hugh Annesley, July 5, 1996, from the United Campaign Against Plastic Bullets, Committee on the Administration of Justice, British Irish Rights Watch, Pat Finucane Centre, Liberty, and the Irish Council for Civil Liberties.

and property, the preservation of the peace and the prevention of crime.[165]

The RUC maintains that the bullets are used only against rioters in situations of serious public disorder, in accord with the principle of minimum use of force. Many of those killed by plastic bullets, however, were subsequently proven not to have been rioting.[166] In each case of death, there has been controversy surrounding the circumstances of the shooting and in many cases eyewitnesses claimed that the use of plastic bullets was completely uncalled for.[167] Testimony taken by Human Rights Watch/Helsinki from numerous plastic bullet victims and witnesses to plastic bullet use during the 1996 marching season strongly indicates that not only were plastic bullets fired indiscriminately, but the injuries reported to us—numerous head and chest injuries—reveal that RUC officers routinely disobeyed internal guidelines for plastic baton round use.[168]

RUC Chief Constable Ronnie Flanagan told Human Rights Watch/Helsinki:

> Nobody abhors the use of plastic baton rounds more than we do. But it is the most appropriate means of crowd control we have available. We've researched gas, we've researched water. I'd like to find something that would work as efficiently as plastic

---

[165]Reply from R. Keatley, Superintendent for Chief Constable, July 11, 1996, RUC Reference: Comm. Sec. 96/361/6.

[166]According to the Committee on the Administration of Justice, "In six cases, a judge or inquest found that those killed were innocent victims. In two further cases involving children aged 10 and 11, no finding of rioting was made by the inquests. In one case, two juries could not agree on whether a victim had been petrol-bombing troops from a kitchen window. In four cases inquest juries judged those killed to have been rioting." See *Plastic Bullets and the Law*, p. 6.

[167]Ibid.

[168]Les Rodgers, chairperson of the Police Federation of Northern Ireland, acknowledged that there had been deaths attributable to plastic bullet use but failed to recognize the bullets themselves as lethal weapons. He told Human Rights Watch/Helsinki, "Plastic bullets are very emotive. People have died but usually the person had a medical condition or a thin bone in the head." Human Rights Watch/Helsinki interview, Belfast, November 25, 1996.

bullets. We are continuously engaged in research. The plastic bullet guns we use are very accurate.[169]

Government and police claims of the selective use, accuracy and efficiency of plastic bullets have been contradicted by scientists and arms experts. Ian Hogg, the editor of *Jane's Counterinsurgency*, a respected defense journal, has challenged the accuracy of the plastic bullet, stating:

> It's just a slab of plastic and with the best will in the world you can't guarantee where it's going to go when you pull the trigger—you do your best to aim at a specific spot but it has no ballistic shape, doesn't spin so it's not stable that way and it will hit and bounce and do all sorts of stupid things.[170]

An International Tribunal of Inquiry into Deaths and Serious Injuries Caused by Plastic Bullets in Northern Ireland, sponsored by the Association for Legal Justice, was held in Belfast in 1981. A follow up inquiry held in 1982, concluded:

> The government has claimed that the plastic bullet was chosen for its improved accuracy. If these claims are accurate, the weapon is being deliberately misused on a large scale. The plastic bullet lends itself to abuse and there has clearly been no attempt to enforce controls, particularly with regard to non-use at short ranges, and aiming only at the lower part of the body.[171]

---

[169]Human Rights Watch/Helsinki interview, Belfast, November 11, 1996.

[170]Cited in Helsinki Watch, *Human Rights in Northern Ireland*, pp. 63-64.

[171]Ibid., p. 12.

The RUC declined our request for a written copy of the force's internal guidelines for the use of plastic bullets.[172] Chief Constable Ronnie Flanagan read from the guidelines to us:

> Plastic bullets are not to be shot at a range of less than twenty meters and are not to be bounced off the ground. They are only to be shot if the safety of police officers or others is seriously threatened. Plastic baton rounds are to be fired only at selected individuals and never indiscriminately at a crowd. They are to be aimed to strike the lower part of the target person's body directly.[173]

Flanagan told Human Rights Watch/Helsinki that he would be "ruthlessly intolerant of anyone going beyond the guidelines although I can't say that every piece of action that every officer engages in is legitimate."[174] Despite the staggering number of plastic bullets fired and the extensive testimony of head and upper body injuries recorded by human rights organizations, including Human Rights Watch/Helsinki, Flanagan claimed there were no cases where senior officers alleged that plastic baton gunners used excessive force during the 1996 marching season.[175] When questioned about the extensive use of the plastic baton round against the Garvaghy Road protesters and at London/Derry from July 11 to 14, 1996, Flanagan told us that he was "proud of the restraint the officers exhibited."[176]

Opponents of plastic bullet use in Northern Ireland also charge that the weapons are used in a sectarian manner, targeting nationalists with greater frequency than unionists. All but one of the fourteen persons killed by plastic

---

[172]This refusal supports the Committee on the Administration of Justice's claim that the police guidelines for plastic bullet use are not in the public domain and that for genuine accountability to be achieved the RUC must make the guidelines public. See *Misrule of Law*, pp. 36-37.

[173]Human Rights Watch/Helsinki interview, Belfast, November 24, 1996.

[174]Ibid.

[175]Ibid. There has been only one prosecution ever of a police officer for firing a fatal plastic bullet shot. See below.

[176]Human Rights Watch/Helsinki interview, Belfast, November 24, 1996.

bullets were Catholics. Claire Reilly of the United Campaign Against Plastic Bullets told Human Rights Watch/Helsinki that "the problem is not only plastic bullets but plastic bullets in the hands of a sectarian police force."[177]

The disparity in the number of plastic bullet firings between the nationalist and unionist communities during July 1996 raises further questions about their sectarian use. During unionist protests in support of the Orange Order stand-off at Drumcree from July 7 to 11, 1996, 662 plastic bullets were fired.[178] When nationalist protests broke out after the Drumcree reversal, over 5,000 plastic bullets were fired from July 11 to 14, 1996.[179] According to RUC statistics, approximately eight times as many plastic bullets were fired in three and a half days of nationalist violence as were fired during four and a half days of violent unionist protest. The Committee on the Administration of Justice has stated:

> Such a disparity clearly raises issues of public concern. . .In particular, the authorities will need to explain why, out of 6,002 bullets fired throughout the period, the situation in Derry/Londonderry required the firing of some 3,006 bullets... CAJ found it difficult to come to any other conclusion than that the security forces were out of control there. Neither the amount of people involved in rioting, nor the threat to life or property, seemed to explain the disproportionate response in the town...No one could justify different police tactics on sectarian grounds. Yet, on the face of it, this may be a difficult charge to refute.[180]

Testimony taken by Human Rights Watch/Helsinki at London/Derry supports the conclusion that, in many incidents where people were injured by plastic bullets, the security forces appeared to be out of control, particularly on the evenings of July 11, 12, and 13, 1996. The number, types and severity of injuries

---

[177]Human Rights Watch/Helsinki interview, Belfast, November 25, 1996.

[178]Committee on the Administration of Justice, *The Misrule of Law*, p. 29.

[179]Ibid., p. 30. This figure is taken from an RUC statement issued on July 19, 1996.

[180]Ibid. The figures noted in the CAJ statement were taken from early estimates made in July 1996 by the RUC itself. As noted above, there were repeated variations in the statistics reported by the RUC.

over a broad demographic sample, coupled with accounts of casualty units being set up in homes to render assistance to hundreds of injured, lead us to conclude that plastic bullet use in many instances was indiscriminate and that the RUC's own guidelines for use were ignored. Moreover, testimony from numerous people indicates that the verbal abuse leveled against nationalists by RUC officers was sectarian in nature and thus lends credence to allegations of the sectarian use of plastic bullets.

Her Majesty's Inspectorate of Constabulary: Plastic Bullet Review
        In the aftermath of Drumcree, Sir Patrick Mayhew, secretary of state for Northern Ireland, requested that Her Majesty's Inspectorate of Constabulary (HMIC), Colin Smith, examine the use of plastic baton rounds by the RUC during the summer of 1996. While there is generally little public confidence in internal governmental reviews of the practices of state agencies,[181] the HMIC report did make a number of admissions and recommendations which imply that RUC officers misused plastic bullets. HMIC's findings include:[182]

•   Due to a serious lapse in public order training, the "overwhelming scale of the disorders that occurred necessitated the deployment of many inadequately trained officers in unprotected vehicles" (6.66).

•   Commitment to the RUC command structure at public order incidents was questioned especially as only a quarter of superintendents have the appropriate training (6.68).

_____

        [181]The Committee on the Administration of Justice criticized the government for making this review part of a routine annual HMIC internal inquiry, "which suggested undue complacency on their part, at the failure to assign this work to an external independent body, and at the failure to open up the inquiry to public scrutiny." CAJ Letter, "Misrule of Law: Update on Recent Developments," November 12, 1996. Indeed, Smith did not consider submissions from interested groups and upon CAJ's invitation to Smith for a meeting to discuss plastic bullet use and the policing of the summer 1996 marches, he replied by letter that his report had been completed. Letter to CAJ from Colin Smith, HMIC, November 5, 1996. HMIC declined to meet with Human Rights Watch/Helsinki in November 1996.

        [182]Northern Ireland Office, *1996 Primary Inspection Royal Ulster Constabulary: A Report of Her Majesty's Inspectorate of Constabulary*, (London: HMSO, 1996). Paragraph numbers from the report follow each finding.

- Some officers were on duty for excessive periods (up to five days) without adequate rest. It is "clearly unsatisfactory to expect officers to remain fully functional under such conditions" (6.69).

- Overall responsibility for the maintenance and development of police response to public disorder is "too fragmented." The present unsatisfactory system for communications between various elements should be improved (6.71).

- HMIC welcomes "confrontational skills training" but criticizes the "very limited input on social skills and defusing situations without resort to the use of force." HMIC urges an increase in "avoidance tactics content" in training (6.74).

- Plastic baton rounds are potentially lethal but developments have aimed at making their use as safe as possible (6.77).

- Reporting procedures for the firing of plastic bullets should include a "clear statement by the senior officer present of his assessment of the potential threat to life from the overall incident."[183] The guidelines for plastic baton round use should have "greater clarity of precision" (6.78).

- Plastic baton round use "should be governed by the formal assessment of intelligence and tension indicators. There is a risk that in those areas where baton guns are routinely issued, they will be treated as a piece of everyday equipment; the issue and potential subsequent use of these weapons should be regarded as a major step, carrying with it the potential to escalate as well as defuse public disorder" (6.82).

HMIC's findings clearly indicate that police response to incidents of large scale public disorder are not only inadequate in terms of resources, training, command structure gaps, and ineffective communications, but also in terms of the use of potentially lethal force as opposed to the development and use of tactical alternatives. Moreover, HMIC's findings obliquely reflect our own conclusion that regular resort to the plastic baton round, coupled with an apparent reluctance to consider alternatives, results in the weapon being wielded and used with an almost casual attitude. The recognition that the use of plastic baton rounds has the

---

[183]Ibid., p. 50.

potential to escalate public disorder is an important one. This finding supports the claims of human rights and community-based organizations that the appearance of plastic baton round gunners is often provocative and can serve to exacerbate an already tense but not yet violent situation.

Although the HMIC report fails to address a number of important policing issues related to the summer's events, it offers a picture of the RUC as a force in need of considerable reform if it is to respond adequately, that is, with the minimum amount of force necessary, to major incidents of public disorder.

Renewing the Call for a Ban on Plastic Bullets

In 1991, Helsinki Watch called for a total ban on the use of plastic baton rounds in Northern Ireland.[184] We joined a long list of organizations and bodies in opposition to the weapon. In 1982, the European Parliament voted to ban the use of plastic bullets throughout the European Community. A technical assistance report on public order and police equipment recently commissioned by the Civil Liberties Committee of the European Parliament is expected to express concern over the continued use of plastic bullets. The British Labour Party's pledge that it would ban the weapon when it resumed leadership of the government can now be tested.[185] A 1986 conference of the Democratic Unionist Party (DUP) criticized the "blatant misuse of the plastic baton round in Portadown" and said the bullet was a "killer weapon, designed to kill or maim."[186] Justice for All, a civil liberties group based in the Shankill area and established to monitor human rights abuses within the Protestant community, strongly criticized the "illegal use of plastic bullets" at the Whiterock Orange Parade in 1993.[187] In 1995, the U.N. Committee Against Torture expressed concern over the continued use of plastic bullets in Northern

---

[184]Helsinki Watch, *Human Rights in Northern Ireland*, p. 67.

[185]National Executive Committee Policy Statement, 1987.

[186]Committee on the Administration of Justice, *Misrule of Law*, p. 25.

[187]Justice for All, *Whiterock Citizens Inquiry* (Belfast, 1993). The inquiry concluded that the "RUC riot squads illegally discharged their plastic baton rounds by aiming their weapons at head height and firing indiscriminately into civilian crowds."

Ireland.[188] The Report of the International Body on Arms Decommissioning, issued in January 1996, called for a review of the use of plastic bullets as a confidence-building measure attendant to the peace negotiations.[189] *The U.S. State Department's Country Reports on Human Rights Practices for 1996* section on the United Kingdom noted the widespread criticism of plastic bullet use by human rights monitors, the European Parliament ban, and the high numbers of head and upper body injuries in spite of RUC guidelines.[190]

Human Rights Watch/Helsinki calls once again for an immediate total ban on the use of plastic bullets in Northern Ireland. The RUC's disproportionate response to the events of the 1996 marching season confirms that plastic bullets frequently were fired indiscriminately, in contravention of the force's internal guidelines, and with an apparently sectarian bias. Plastic bullets were often fired in situations where there was no threat to officers, residents, or property. It is incumbent on the government of the United Kingdom to find alternative means of crowd control for the protection of officers and members of the public.[191]

The Requirements of International Law
        The policing of contentious marches in Northern Ireland raises a number of concerns about the United Kingdom's obligations under international law. International codes of conduct provide universally endorsed guidelines for police accountability[192] and the use of force by law enforcement officials. Guidelines

---

[188]U.N. Committee Against Torture, *Consideration of Second Periodic Report of the United Kingdom of Great Britain and Northern Ireland*, November 17, 1995, paras. 36, 55.

[189]*Report of the International Body on Arms Decommissioning*, January 24, 1996, para. 55.

[190] *U.S. Department of State Country Reports on Human Rights Practices for 1996*, February 1997, pp. 1191-1201.

[191]See Quaker Council for European Affairs, *Crowd Control: Are There Alternatives to Violence? A Study of Methods of Crowd Control in the Member States of the Council of Europe*, May 1986.

[192]The United Nations Code of Conduct for Law Enforcement Officials includes provisions on police accountability for compliance with international standards. Article 2 requires police to uphold the human rights of all persons in the performance of their duties. These rights are enumerated in major human rights treaties including the International

regulating the use of force are particularly relevant in assessing the use of plastic bullets and allegations of police brutality on the Garvaghy Road and in London/Derry in July 1996.

The marching phenomenon itself is governed by a number of internationally recognized human rights guarantees which provide protections for peaceful assemblies and for members of the communities through which they march. The ultimate balancing of the interests of both communities in the political context of the Northern Ireland conflict is a complex exercise and one that generally is beyond the mandate of Human Rights Watch/Helsinki to comment upon. However, with respect to the management of contentious marches, some conclusions are appropriate in cases where public safety is seriously at risk due to marchers who credibly threaten or actually use violence as a means to guarantee that a march proceeds or in the course of a march. Likewise, in cases where protesters credibly threaten to perpetrate acts of violence upon marchers, authorities may take measures to proscribe certain activities in the interest of public safety. Furthermore, in the event that a march can be characterized as a peaceful assembly, some observations are appropriate in cases where certain guaranteed rights of individuals are wholly abrogated in order that the guaranteed rights of others might be exercised.

The Use of Force

Concerns arose throughout the summer of 1996 about the RUC's resort to the use of force, and the nature and extent of the force used, particularly with respect to the use of plastic bullets. Domestic criminal law in Northern Ireland provides a lower standard for the use of force than international codes of conduct and human rights treaties to which the United Kingdom is a party.

Section 3(1) of the Criminal Law (Northern Ireland) Act 1967 states that law enforcement officials may use "such force as is reasonable under the circumstances in the prevention of crime, or in effecting or assisting in the lawful arrest of offenders." Few police officers have been held liable under this standard because of the broad interpretation the courts have given "reasonable under the circumstances," especially in the context of anti-terrorism and public order policing measures employed by the RUC throughout the conflict. A 1991 Helsinki Watch mission to Northern Ireland found that the "reasonableness" standard provided too

---

Covenant on Civil and Political Rights, to which the U.K. is a party. Article 8 requires law enforcement officials to report violations or known impending violations of the code to the appropriate authorities or state agencies "vested with reviewing or remedial power." G.A. res. 34/169, annex, 34 U.N. GAOR Supp. (No. 46) at 186, U.N. Doc. A/34/46 (1979).

much leeway for the police and army to use excessive force and "inevitably leads to abuses."[193]   Helsinki Watch recommended then that the standard for the use of force should be "absolute necessity" as grounded in international standards and codes.[194]

The "necessity" standard for the use of force by law enforcement officials and security forces is well-established in international law. In the International Covenant on Civil and Political Rights (ICCPR) the standard is articulated as a prohibition on the "arbitrary" deprivation of life and in the European Convention for the Protection of Human Rights and Fundamental Freedoms (ECHR) the standard is articulated as a guarantee that persons shall not be deprived of the right to life by the use of force unless such force is absolutely necessary. Specifically, article 2 of the ECHR states that "Deprivation of life shall not be regarded as inflicted in contravention of this Article when it results from the use of force which is no more than absolutely necessary." The ECHR standard is particularly relevant to several of the fourteen cases of persons killed by plastic bullets in Northern Ireland.[195]

The United Nations Code of Conduct for Law Enforcement Officials states that "Law enforcement officials may use force only when strictly necessary

---

[193]Helsinki Watch, *Human Rights in Northern Ireland*, p. 59.

[194]Ibid.

[195]There has been only one prosecution of a police officer for the lethal firing of a plastic bullet. Twenty-two-year-old Sean Downes was shot and killed at an internment rally in 1984. The judge held that the RUC's internal guidelines for plastic bullet use had not been followed: Downes had been hit in the chest and the bullet had been fired from less than twenty meters. The officer said in his defense that he fired to protect two fellow officers toward whom Downes was running with a stick. The officer was acquitted. The judge ruled that the accused acted "almost instinctively to defend his comrades without having time to assess the situation in light of his knowledge of the police regulations." See Helsinki Watch, *Human Rights in Northern Ireland*, p. 65. The jurisprudence in Northern Ireland thus interprets the "reasonableness" standard as a subjective measure requiring an assessment of the state of mind of the offending officer. The international standard of "absolute necessity" governed by the principle of proportionality is an objective standard under which subjective states of mind are not dispositive.

and to the extent required for the performance of their duty."[196] The official commentary to the code states:

> (a) This provision emphasizes that the use of force by law enforcement officials should be exceptional; while it implies that law enforcement officials may be authorized to use force as is reasonably necessary under the circumstances for the prevention of crime or in effecting or assisting in the lawful arrest of offenders or suspected offenders, no force beyond that may be used.
>
> (b) National law ordinarily restricts the use of force by law enforcement officials in accordance with a principle of proportionality. It is to be understood that such national principles of proportionality are to be respected in the interpretation of this provision. In no case should this provision be interpreted to authorize the use of force which is disproportionate to the legitimate objective to be achieved.

The United Nations Basic Principles on the Use of Force and Firearms by Law Enforcement Officials[197] serves as a guide for the more effective implementation of the Code of Conduct for Law Enforcement Officials. The second general provision urges governments to develop "non-lethal incapacitating weapons for use in appropriate situations with a view to increasingly restraining the application of means capable of causing death or injury to persons." Other relevant provisions include:

> 4. Law enforcement officials, in carrying out their duty, shall, as far as possible, apply non-violent means before resorting to the use of force and firearms. They may use force and firearms only

---

[196]Code of Conduct for Law Enforcement Officials , G.A. res. 34/169, annex, 34 U.N. GAOR Supp. (No. 46) at 186, U.N. Doc. A/34/46 (1979).

[197]Basic Principles on the Use of Force and Firearms by Law Enforcement Officials, Eighth United Nations Congress on the Prevention of Crime and the Treatment of Offenders, Havana, 27 August to 7 September 1990, U.N. Doc. A/CONF.144/28/rev.1 at 112 (1990).

if other means remain ineffective or without any promise of achieving the intended result.

5. Whenever the lawful use of force and firearms is unavoidable, law enforcement officials shall:
> (a) exercise restraint in such use and act in proportion to the seriousness of the offense and the legitimate objective to be achieved;
> (b) Minimize damage and injury, and respect and preserve life. . .

Notably, general provision eight states that "exceptional circumstances such as political instability or any other public emergency may not be invoked to justify any departure from these basic principles." Thus, the expansive police powers enjoyed by the RUC under emergency legislation do not release law enforcement officials from the responsibility to carry out their duties according to the internationally recognized principle of necessity.

Human Rights Watch/Helsinki concludes that the "reasonableness" standard for the use of force in Northern Ireland should be replaced by the standard of "necessity" as grounded in international standards and codes of conduct. This requires that force used must be in proportion to the actual danger presented and not based on the subjective assessment of danger as determined by individual police officers. Furthermore, we conclude that under both the domestic "reasonableness" standard and the international "necessity" standard, the RUC used excessive force when removing protesters from the Garvaghy Road in Portadown and in the use of plastic bullets on Garvaghy Road protesters and at many citizens of London/Derry in July 1996.

Marching, Public Safety, and the Balancing of Rights

The right to peaceful assembly, and by extension the right to march, is guaranteed by the ICCPR and the ECHR both of which are binding on the United Kingdom. ICCPR article 21 states:

> The right of peaceful assembly shall be recognized. No restrictions may be placed on the exercise of this right other than those imposed in conformity with the law and which are

necessary in a democratic society in the interests of national security or public safety, public order (*ordre public*), the protection of public health or morals or the protection of the rights and freedoms of others.

Article 11 of the ECHR states:

1. Everyone has the right to freedom of peaceful assembly and to freedom of association with others, including the right to form and to join trade unions for the protection of his interests.

2. No restrictions shall be placed on the exercise of these rights other than such as are prescribed by law and are necessary in a democratic society in the interests of national security or public safety, for the prevention of disorder or crime, for the protection of health or morals or for the protection of the rights and freedoms of others. This Article shall not prevent the imposition of lawful restrictions on these rights by members of the armed forces, of the police or of the administration of the State.

The right to free assembly is rooted firmly in universally recognized democratic principles. Assemblies, marches and demonstrations typically are used for the collective exercise of the right to freedom of expression. As one commentator notes, the "discourse of conflicting ideas is an essential feature of democracy."[198] Therefore, state interference with the right to freedom of assembly must be exceptional. Limitations on assembly must be imposed in conformity with law and must be necessary—that is, proportional—to protecting one of the enumerated interests (i.e. national security, public safety, public order, protection of the rights of others). Limitations also must be *necessary in a democratic society* for attaining one of the enumerated purposes. Notably, it is the principle of democracy which governs the exercise of the right to peaceful assembly *and* the limitations on the right.

Human Rights Watch/Helsinki has a strong commitment to freedom of expression and freedom of assembly as core principles of human rights. We therefore generally view as suspect any action by a government to proscribe any expression short of incitement to illegal action or to place restrictions on any

---

[198]Manfred Nowak, *U.N. Covenant on Civil and Political Rights: CCPR Commentary* (Kehl, Strasbourg, Arlington: N.P. Engel, 1993), p. 381.

assembly unless members of that assembly threaten imminent violence. Thus, expression generally should never be punished nor peaceful assemblies restricted for their subject matter or content alone, no matter how offensive it may be to others.

However, claims by the RUC that the situation at Drumcree was "dangerous," that the decision was made to permit the march because there was a "real, imminent, pressing threat to life," and that Northern Ireland was "at as dangerous a position as at any time in thirty years" are powerful indicators that state authorities had knowledge that the marchers threatened imminent violence. The fact that these acts apparently were aimed at guaranteeing that the march would proceed did little to dispel fears that violence, targeted at the minority community which had sought government protection, could ensue in the course of the march. Indeed, as amply documented above, many acts of violence had already been committed by supporters of the Orange Order's demand to walk down the Garvaghy Road when the RUC took the decision to allow the march to proceed. That a demonstration already responsible for inciting violence and perpetrating acts of violence was allowed to proceed into a minority community raises serious concerns about the authorities' commitment to protect the rights of that minority.

The RUC also told Human Rights Watch/Helsinki that severe restrictions were placed on Lower Ormeau residents in order to protect them. RUC Chief Constable Ronnie Flanagan claimed that the Lower Ormeau Road had the potential to be more contentious than Drumcree and that if the Orange Order were not permitted to proceed down the road, serious violence would have erupted.[199] Flanagan stated:

> Don't let me understate the objectionable nature of such a heavy presence in such a small area. But it was as serious a time as I've seen. There was a risk of this degenerating into a civil war. We took heavy preventive measures based on intelligence not available to you. It was a "benign siege" in light of perhaps a more "malevolent siege" that would have happened if Drumcree was transferred to the Lower Ormeau.[200]

The essence of the right to free assembly is challenged by these RUC assertions: if the Orange Order presented a violent threat to the community, were

---

[199]Human Rights Watch/Helsinki interview, Belfast, November 11, 1996.

[200]Ibid.

the assemblies "peaceful" as contemplated by the ICCPR and the ECHR? If the assemblies were not, in fact, peaceful and the RUC had knowledge that violence was imminent, it was incumbent upon the police to place restrictions on the march, not solely on the community (members of which may also have planned violence). It is well-established in international law that the right to assembly may be restricted in the interest of public safety:

> An assembly may be restricted, prohibited and, if necessary, broken up to protect public safety when it constitutes a specific threat to the safety of persons (i.e. their lives, their physical integrity or health) or things. This is, e.g., the case when, as a result of clashes between opposing groups, the police are no longer in a position to guarantee the physical safety of demonstrators or passers-by or when a demonstration leads to the plundering of businesses. Whereas in these cases the assembly is usually no longer peaceful within the meaning of Article 21, preventive assembly prohibitions may also be necessary under certain circumstances to protect public safety.[201]

Given the credible threat of violence, particularly in light of widespread unionist violence during the Drumcree stand-off, the RUC would have been in compliance with international law if it had taken steps to restrict these marches in the interest of public safety. By failing to address the violence at its origins, the RUC helped create the debacle that became "Drumcree" and proceeded to contribute to a repeat of the events at Drumcree by submitting to threats of violence on the Lower Ormeau Road.

It is important to note that in interviews with Human Rights Watch/Helsinki, the RUC generally focused its claims of "protection" on the communities through which the Orangemen were to march. The threat thus appeared to come from the marchers, those claiming a right to peaceful assembly but advancing that right by violent means. However, restrictive measures may also be placed on protesters and those in opposition to marches if they threaten imminent violence.

Assuming, for the sake of argument, that the march on the Lower Ormeau Road was, in fact, a peaceful assembly threatening no risk of violence to community, the principle of proportionality requires that any interference with the right to free assembly must be necessary to achieve one of the enumerated

---

[201]Nowak, *CCPR Commentary*, p. 380

purposes. Thus, where the exercise of the right to free assembly infringes on the rights and freedoms of others, only limitations proportionate to the protection of the rights of others can be imposed on the assembly. The police are under a double duty to protect the rights of those assembled *and* to guarantee that the rights of others are not violated in the process.[202] Where the rights of others are fundamental civil and political freedoms, any limitations also must be narrowly tailored to protect the right of assembly to the greatest possible extent.

The total hemming in of the nationalist community on the Lower Ormeau Road by the RUC on July 11 to 12, 1996, resulted in the violation of a number of internationally guaranteed rights, including the right to freedom of movement and the right to privacy. Article 12 of the ICCPR states:

> 1. Everyone lawfully within the territory of a State shall, within that territory, have the right to liberty of movement and freedom to choose his residence.
>
> 3. The above-mentioned rights shall not be subject to any restrictions except those which are provided by law, are necessary to protect national security, public order (*ordre public*), public health or morals or the rights and freedoms of others, and are consistent with the other rights recognized in the present Covenant.[203]

Restrictions on freedom of movement are governed by the principle of proportionality which requires a precise balancing between the right to freedom of movement and those interests to be protected by the interference. Only those interests enumerated in article 12(3) justify interference with freedom of

---

[202]Under European law, the general formula for assessing the permissibility of limitations on free expression and association rights involves a number of factors. According to Harris, O'Boyle and Warbrick, these include: the importance of the protected right, the need in a democratic society to promote tolerance and broad-mindedness, the weight and significance of the interests that the state is seeking to protect by interfering with the protected right, and the notion that the state must act proportionately in seeking to strike the correct balance between competing rights. See D.J. Harris, M. O'Boyle, and C. Warbrick, *Law of the European Convention on Human Rights* (London:Butterworths, 1995).

[203]Article 2 of the Fourth Protocol to the ECHR guarantees essentially the same right to freedom of movement as article 12 of ICCPR.

movement. A United Nations draft declaration on freedom of movement defines a restriction on movement as necessary "only if it responds to a pressing public and social need, pursues a legitimate aim and is proportionate to that aim."[204]

The right to privacy is guaranteed by article 17 of the ICCPR:

> 1. No one shall be subjected to arbitrary or unlawful interference with his privacy, family, home or correspondence, nor to unlawful attacks on his honour and reputation.
>
> 2. Everyone has the right to the protection of the law against such interference or attacks.

"Arbitrary interference" has been interpreted as action by state authorities containing "elements of injustice, unpredictability, and unreasonableness."[205] State interference with the right to privacy is also governed by the principle of proportionality which requires the balancing of the right with the state interest advanced by limiting the right.

Employing a "balancing of rights" approach, the events of July 11 to 12, 1996, on the Lower Ormeau Road apparently present a competition between members of the Orange Order seeking to exercise their rights to free expression and assembly by marching down the road versus community members seeking to exercise their rights to freedom of movement and the right to privacy. As noted above, primary responsibility for ensuring that the rights of others are not unduly infringed by the exercise of any other internationally guaranteed right rests with state authorities and is governed by the principle of proportionality. Thus, the question under review is: were the measures taken by the RUC with respect to the hemming in of the Lower Ormeau community necessary to protect the right of the marchers to exercise their right to free assembly?

Human Rights Watch/Helsinki concludes that the principle of proportionality was violated by the RUC on the Lower Ormeau Road. The RUC

---

[204]*Draft Declaration on Freedom and Non-Discrimination in Respect of the Right of Everyone to Leave Any Country, Including His Own, and to Return to His Country* in CLC Mubanga-Chipoya, "Analysis of the Current Trends and Developments Regarding the Right to Leave Any Country Including One's Own, and to Return to One's Own Country, and Some Other Rights or Consideration Arising Therefrom," E/CN.4/Sub.2/1987/10, Annex I, p. 50.

[205]Nowak, *CCPR Commentary*, p. 292.

made operational decisions which resulted in the total abrogation of the rights to freedom of movement and privacy for many residents of the Lower Ormeau community so that the Orange Order could exercise its right to march. Some Lower Ormeau residents were prohibited from access to their homes and jobs, from essentials such as food and medical treatment, and—perhaps most egregiously — from access to their children, the elderly, and the infirm. Indeed, some residents were confined in their homes or other buildings, as if under house arrest. The interest to be protected by these measures, the right to free assembly, is not absolute and it cannot be said that measures necessary to protect its exercise are warranted without qualification.

By asserting that the measures taken by the RUC were disproportionate, Human Rights Watch/Helsinki does not argue that the march itself should not have progressed. The police were under a duty to strike a balance between the marchers' right to assemble and the residents' rights to movement and privacy that, insofar as possible, allowed for the least intrusion on the exercise of each right rather than a wholesale abrogation of one group's rights to vindicate those of the other group. An effort to achieve such balance was not even attempted by the RUC. Some limitations on movement probably would have been justified as is usually the case when large public processions utilize public roads. A cordon around the entire community with a virtual ban on movement, however, was unwarranted and potentially dangerous for many residents and their families.

August 1996: A Briefing on Marching Events at Dunloy and London/Derry

Every August, the Apprentice Boys of Derry commemorate the Siege of Derry, that is, the closing of the London/Derry city gates by the apprentice boys in 1688, and the relief of the siege in August 1689.[206] On August 12, 1995, an Apprentice Boys march around the walls surrounding the London/Derry city center was accompanied by a heavy police presence. The RUC and nationalist protesters clashed. Nationalists charged that the RUC used excessive physical force, indiscriminately shot plastic bullets, and used sectarian language throughout the police operation.[207]

On August 7, 1996, in the aftermath of Drumcree—and after attempts at accommodation between the Bogside Residents Group (BRG) and the Apprentice

---

[206]Jarman and Bryan, *Parade and Protest*, p. 11.

[207]Pat Finucane Centre, *One Day in August: The Report of the Pat Finucane Centre into the Allegations of the Abuse of Human Rights Arising out of the Apprentice Boys Parade in Derry City on August 12th 1995*, August 28, 1995, p. 5.

Boys failed—Sir Patrick Mayhew, the secretary of state for Northern Ireland, banned all marches, including the Apprentice Boys' annual march, from a section of the city walls between Bishop's Gate and Magazine Gate, overlooking the Bogside, a predominantly nationalist community. Sir Patrick stated that he made the decision on the advice of RUC Chief Constable Hugh Annesley who told Mayhew that the Apprentice Boys march was likely to place "undue demands" on the police force.[208] The Apprentice Boys held a parade and marched through London/Derry city center but stayed off the walls. According to William Moore of the Apprentice Boys, "because we couldn't walk that section, we decided not to walk at all but would walk at a time of our own choosing."[209] The Apprentice Boys walked the walls of London/Derry on October 19, 1996. The BRG mounted a symbolic protest and two protesters were removed from the walls by the RUC. SDLP leader John Hume spoke out on October 18, 1996, in the *Irish News*, in favor of protecting the civil liberties of the Apprentice Boys and allowing the march to proceed.

In the small nationalist village of Dunloy, approximately fifty Apprentice Boys sought to march through the town center on the morning of August 10, 1996, on their way to the main Apprentice Boys march in London/Derry.[210] Residents of Dunloy threatened the marchers with hurley sticks and the RUC took a decision to prohibit the marchers from marching through Dunloy. The marchers boarded their bus and quit Dunloy but promised to return that evening. Members of the Dunloy Residents and Parents Association (DRPA) met with the RUC and brokered a deal whereby the Apprentice Boys would be allowed access to their hall in Dunloy but would not be allowed to march through the town.[211]

In the early evening hundreds of Apprentice Boys descended on Dunloy demanding the right to march. Christine Bell, chairperson of the Committee for the

---

[208]Seamus McKinney, "Army Closes off the Walls in 'Surprise' NIO Decision," *Irish News*, August 8, 1996.

[209]Human Rights Watch/Helsinki interview, London/Derry, November 7, 1996.

[210]The Dunloy march would have been one of a number of smaller "feeder" marches which are held in the morning in towns and cities across Northern Ireland and whose participants then proceed to London/Derry, usually by bus, to participate in the main march of the walls and through the center of London/Derry city.

[211]Human Rights Watch/Helsinki interview, Dunloy, November 10, 1996.

Administration of Justice, was an observer at Dunloy. She told Human Rights Watch/Helsinki:

> At 6:00 p.m. that same day [August 10] many busloads of people returning from the Apprentice Boys march in Derry stopped at Dunloy and tried to march. Many of them were drunk. The townspeople panicked because they had little trust for the police because of what happened on the Garvaghy Road. The marchers almost broke through the police lines. The police appeared to panic and tried to get riot gear on. I've never run so hard in my life. There were hundreds of angry people and the police prevented them from marching into the town. The police acted well but were under-resourced and used plastic bullets against the Apprentice Boys.[212]

Ronnie Flanagan, then deputy chief constable, flew in from Belfast to oversee the police operation.[213] The police held the Apprentice Boys and eventually the crowd dissipated and quit Dunloy for the second time that day. According to Tony Shivers of the Dunloy Residents and Parents Association, "if the police hadn't been there that day there would've been murder."[214] Although Dunloy residents were generally critical of the RUC, members of the DRPA made the following comments about the work of the RUC at Dunloy on August 10, 1996:[215]

> * "To their credit, they kept law and order."
> * "You would have to say they did a good job."
> * "They earned some credit for doing their job."

---

[212]Human Rights Watch/Helsinki telephone interview, November 6, 1996.

[213]Human Rights Watch/Helsinki interview with Ronnie Flanagan, Belfast, November 11, 1996.

[214]Human Rights Watch/Helsinki interview, Dunloy, November 10, 1996.

[215]Human Rights Watch/Helsinki interview with Anne Martin, Paddy O'Kane, Tony Shivers, Patsy Scott, and John McQuillan of the Dunloy Residents and Parents Association, Dunloy, November 10, 1996.

It remains unclear why the government and the RUC took such dramatically different approaches to public order and contentious marches in August 1996 than it did in July 1996. When Human Rights Watch/Helsinki queried John Steele of the Northern Ireland Office (NIO) as to why the secretary of state did not ban the march at Drumcree in July, he responded: "Because the chief constable didn't ask the secretary of state to ban the march at Drumcree."[216] It is profoundly disturbing that the NIO placed responsibility for a public order crisis amounting to the worst violence in Northern Ireland in nearly two decades with an unelected senior police officer who simply failed to make a request for a ban.

Independent Review of Parades and Marches

In July 1996, Sir Patrick Mayhew announced the establishment of the Independent Review of Parades and Marches to evaluate the current arrangements for handling public processions and open-air public meetings and associated public order issues in Northern Ireland. The Independent Review consisted of a three member, all male board: Dr. Peter North, chairperson and vice-chancellor of Oxford University; Rev. John Dunlop, a Presbyterian minister, writer and lecturer; and Father Oliver Crilly, a Catholic priest from Strabane, County Tyrone. The Independent Review conducted over ninety meetings, including sessions with the NIO, the RUC, political parties, nongovernmental organizations (including Human Rights Watch/Helsinki), fraternal orders, and residents groups, and received hundreds of written submissions. Its final recommendations, issued on January 30, 1997, included:[217]

- The establishment of a five member Parades Commission for Northern Ireland, with members appointed by the secretary of state, which would create a code of conduct for marchers and protesters, facilitate local mediation of contentious parades, and determine what conditions might be imposed on marches and parades in the absence of local accommodation. The chief constable, however, would have the right to appeal any decision made by the Parades Commission to the secretary of state and the police would retain the ability to intervene in any public procession on public order grounds, as a parade is assembling or

---

[216]Human Rights Watch/Helsinki interview, Belfast, November 12, 1996.

[217]This information is taken from "Summary of Recommendations," *Report of the Independent Review of Parades and Marches*, pp. 205-211.

proceeding. The Parades Commission has been established but it has not yet been invested with the ability to make determinations with respect to conditions on contentious marches. Currently, the commission is meeting with a variety groups and facilitating mediation.

•   A new offense created to penalize individuals who set out deliberately through force of numbers or threat of disorder to contravene the legal determination of the Parades Commission, in defiance of its authority.

•   An extension of the notice requirement for all marches from seven to twenty-one days.

•   The banning of alcohol at all marches and parades.[218]

Human Rights Watch/Helsinki welcomes the establishment of the Parades Commission but is troubled by the failure of the Independent Review to evaluate the policing of marches and parades in its final report. The report presumes that the violence of the summer of 1996 was a result solely of intercommunal conflict and makes its recommendations based on that presumption. Little critique of police operations, possible police misconduct, or accountability for the government, the RUC, or the Police Authority with respect to the summer's events appears in the report. This absence of attention to policing, coupled with the recommendation that the RUC retain the power to intervene in marches on public order grounds and to appeal the Parades Commission's decisions to the secretary of state, once again leaves the RUC in the enviable position of being accountable to no one, except itself.[219]

---

[218]The banning of alcohol and the change in notice requirements were implemented in May 1997 by the new government.

[219]On May 14, 1997, the new government announced that it would bring forward legislation which would fully implement the Independent Review's recommendation that the Parades Commission have responsibility for determining the conditions under which marches proceed. The legislation will not be implemented in time for the summer 1997 marching season, thus the RUC retains jurisdiction over marches for the upcoming season. It is unclear what powers the RUC will have under this new legislation. If the purpose of the law is simply to implement the Independent Review's recommendations, as noted above, the RUC will still retain significant powers over public processions in Northern Ireland.

5. PARAMILITARY "POLICING:" PUNISHMENT ATTACKS AND EXPULSION ORDERS

Introduction

Throughout "the Troubles" in Northern Ireland, the police have concentrated their efforts on the suppression of political violence by paramilitary groups. This anti-terrorist campaign has been waged to the exclusion of many traditional policing functions in some areas. For example, in many nationalist communities, routine foot patrols were rare and RUC land rover patrols were often backed up by British military vehicles. Both nationalists and unionists have alleged that the RUC did not respond to calls requesting assistance with ordinary crimes or, if the police did respond, officers would pick up "suspects" in an attempt to persuade them to serve as political informers.[220] In addition, the RUC has enjoyed expansive police powers under Northern Ireland's emergency legislation[221] further contributing to the notion that the RUC is not a traditional police force charged primarily with the duty to respond to common crime.

During the paramilitary cease-fires, the RUC did take the opportunity to highlight and publicize anti-drug education programs in schools and domestic violence initiatives. Foot patrols, absent the heavy military presence, were also established in some areas of Northern Ireland, including Belfast and London/Derry. These efforts were viewed with suspicion by many nationalists as a superficial "charm offensive" masking the true nature of the RUC as a counterinsurgency force whose principal activity remained rooting out republican "terrorists."[222] Whether or not the RUC's efforts during the cease fires were genuine, research undertaken

---

[220]See Human Rights Watch/Helsinki, *Children in Northern Ireland: Abused by Security Forces and Paramilitaries* (New York: Human Rights Watch, 1992).

[221]See chapter one in this report for a review of police powers under the existing emergency legislation in Northern Ireland.

[222] Then Chief Constable Hugh Annesley noted that the RUC had taken steps to respond to the cease-fires but cautioned that since terrorist organizations were still intact, "the RUC had to strike a balance between being ready and able to protect the community again if necessary, while at the same time ensuring that we responded positively to the changing situation." See *The Chief Constable's Annual Report: Royal Ulster Constabulary 1995*, June 1996, p. 13. This comment is striking for its singular notion of what protecting the community entails, that is, protecting the community from terrorists. The ambivalence in the comment was clearly communicated to communities in which paramilitary groups operate.

by Human Rights Watch/Helsinki indicates that many communities in Northern Ireland do not enjoy a traditional police service invested with the primary duty to assist the community with ordinary crime. In these communities, many normal policing functions have been abandoned. Moreover, in the post-cease-fire period, many of the policing initiatives claimed by the RUC as attempts at the "normalization" of policing have been sacrificed as anti-terrorism security measures have intensified.[223]

In the absence of normal policing, both republican and loyalist paramilitary organizations have assumed a quasi-policing role in their respective communities by meting out "punishments"[224] for perceived or actual offenses, such as drug trafficking, burglary, assault, wife abuse, glue sniffing, public intoxication, joyriding (the reckless driving of stolen cars) and other "anti-social" activities; in other words, non-political offenses normally dealt with through routine policing by a traditional police force. Paramilitary punishments take a variety of forms, including summary executions, crippling shootings, and brutal beatings by paramilitary volunteers against members of their own communities. "Expulsion" orders are also issued by paramilitary organizations to force an alleged perpetrator to leave a particular city or all of Northern Ireland for a designated period of time.

The IRA and loyalist paramilitary groups such as the Ulster Defense Association (UDA) and Ulster Volunteer Force (UVF) operate parallel unofficial criminal justice systems in the vacuum left by the police. Paramilitary organizations act as investigator, prosecutor, judge and jury, and they carry out their own sentences. Warnings are sometimes given before shootings or beatings but even crude due process guarantees are generally dispensed with in favor of summary proceedings. The paramilitaries label these activities "community policing" but this term is a euphemism for brutal punishment techniques which force people in some communities to live in fear under paramilitary control.

During the cease-fires, punishment beatings in both communities rose dramatically. In its January 1996 report, the International Body on Arms

---

[223]Deric Henderson and Ian Graham, "Antiterrorist Measures Increased After IRA Bomb Alert," *London Press Association News,* FBIS-TOT-97-012-L, January 10, 1997.

[224]The term "punishment" as applied to these practices is an imprecise term. As Liam Kennedy notes, "Not only has the label 'punishment' a euphemistic quality when applied to extremely cruel practices, it also carries a presumption that the victim is somehow deserving of what he (occasionally she) receives." In "Nightmares within Nightmares: Paramilitary Repression within Working Class Communities," *Crime and Punishment in West Belfast* (West Belfast: The Summer School, 1995), p. 86, fn. 2.

Decommissioning, chaired by former U.S. Senator George Mitchell, condemned punishment attacks stating:

> We join the Governments, religious leaders and many others in condemning "punishment" killings and attacks. They contribute to the fear that those who have used violence to pursue political objectives in the past will do so again in the future. Such actions have no place in a lawful society.[225]

One of the six "Mitchell Principles" governing the conduct of parties to the peace negotiations recommended that all parties commit themselves to urge that punishment attacks stop and to take effective steps to prevent such attacks.[226] The fact that the cessation of punishment attacks is one of six core recommendations in a report widely believed to be the blueprint for the progression of peace negotiations in Northern Ireland demonstrates that this phenomenon is a political and social problem of magnitude.

Human Rights Watch/Helsinki spoke with political leaders, RUC management, police officers, social workers, probation officers, former paramilitaries, victims of punishment shootings and beatings, and the relatives of victims about the nature of policing in their communities and the establishment of unofficial "criminal justice" systems by paramilitary organizations.[227] We interviewed members of both the nationalist and unionist communities who admitted that they do not call the police when crimes occur because they suspect that the RUC will not respond or will respond inappropriately, for example, by ignoring their call for assistance and attempting solely to employ the complainant or the alleged perpetrator as a political informer. Despite this general suspicion,

---

[225]*Report of the International Body on Arms Decommissioning*, January 24, 1996, para. 21. This body was established to provide an "independent assessment" of the possibilities for the decommissioning of paramilitary weapons. Decommissioning is the second track of a "twin track process" leading up to peace negotiations. The second track, the "political track," invites all political parties to participate in preparatory talks "on the basis, participation, structure, format, and agenda" for substantive peace negotiations.

[226]Ibid., para. 20. The International Body also included Gen. John de Chastelain, from Canada, and Mr. Harri Holkeri, from Finland.

[227]Many of the persons with whom Human Rights Watch/Helsinki spoke cannot be named, nor can their organizations, for fear of paramilitary retribution.

the public's response to the rise of alternative justice systems is varied; many residents resoundingly condemn them but some applaud the efforts of the paramilitaries to protect the community from "anti-social" elements.

Abrogation by the Royal Ulster Constabulary (RUC) of Normal Policing

It is undisputed that policing in Northern Ireland is a dangerous enterprise. Two hundred and ninety-eight police officers have been killed since 1969. Countless others have been physically wounded and psychologically scarred by the political violence. Police officers fear that calls from some troubled areas are "traps," especially in light of the end of the IRA cease-fire and the full-scale resumption of violence by republican paramilitaries. Despite these legitimate concerns, it is incumbent upon the RUC to offer normal policing services in every community. Otherwise, the alternative "criminal justice" systems established by the paramilitaries will continue unjustly to brutalize the people of Northern Ireland.

Prior to the paramilitary cease-fires in 1994, the RUC acknowledged that it did not carry out normal policing in certain parts of Northern Ireland. The RUC claimed:

> The level of terrorist threat, the possibility of ambushes, and the terrorists' well-documented disregard for the safety of local people when mounting such attacks against police officers and soldiers all necessitate caution. This inevitably has resulted in the RUC not being able to respond on occasion, and in specific areas, as quickly as either they or the public would wish.[228]

Hugh Annesley, the RUC chief constable who retired in August 1996, has stated that:

> It is a fact, a highly regrettable fact, that terrorism has distorted policing, to the disadvantage of the community and the Police - and against the desires of both. Necessary security measures have adversely affected policing methods; the terrorist threat has inhibited the degree and quality of contact between the Police

---

[228]Cited in BBC television documentary "Dispatches" by Malachi O'Doherty, broadcast in February 1992. See also Human Rights Watch/Helsinki, *Children in Northern Ireland*, pp. 34-35.

and the public and, at times and in places, the nature of the Police response to community needs.[229]

RUC Chief Constable Ronnie Flanagan, who assumed his position in November 1996, has echoed Annesley's comments. Flanagan told Human Rights Watch/Helsinki that prior to the cease-fires, "we were forced by the situation to wear flak jackets and to drive land rovers. This created unwanted barriers between us and the community."[230] Flanagan claimed that since the cease-fires,[231] there are no more "no go" areas for the RUC.[232] But he also claimed that "we've been able to confine 'the troubles' to relatively small areas that are readily identifiable."[233] Les Rodgers, chairman of the Police Federation of Northern Ireland and a twenty-five-year veteran of the RUC, also told the mission that "the RUC goes everywhere."[234] He immediately conditioned this statement by adding:

But bear in mind the security situation. During the cease-fire, police went out without flak jackets, on foot. After the cease-

---

[229]Address to the Armagh Diocesan Synod, October 22, 1991, p. 5.

[230]Human Rights Watch/Helsinki interview, Belfast, November 11, 1996.

[231]Human Rights Watch/Helsinki interviewed RUC Chief Constable Ronnie Flanagan in November 1996. The IRA cease fire had ended; in England with the February 1996 bombing at Canary Wharf and in Northern Ireland with the October 1996 bombing of British army barracks at Lisburn. It was not until January 1997 that the IRA issued a New Year's statement in the Republican newspaper *An Phoblacht* reaffirming its "steadfast commitment" to the republican objective of reunifying the North with the Republic of Ireland. This statement was widely perceived as the IRA's confirmation of the resumption of full scale military operations in this pursuit. See "IRA 'Unified, Confident, and Steadfast,'" *An Phoblacht/Republican News*, January 9, 1997.

[232] At the beginning of "the troubles," "no-go" areas were established and controlled by republican paramilitaries. These areas, mainly in Belfast and London/Derry, were "liberated" from the police and the British army from 1969 until 1972 when the army reestablished control over them. See Mark Urban, *Big Boys' Rules: The Secret Struggle Against the IRA* (London: Faber and Faber, 1992), p. 15.

[233]Human Rights Watch/Helsinki interview, November 11, 1996.

[234]Human Rights Watch/Helsinki interview, November 25, 1996.

fire, officers were in self-preservation mode. There is a real fear
of ambush. That's why you have to be very careful. It's a simple
fact: if you have intelligence of ambush, you simply don't go. In
other places, police officers are killed incidental to crimes. In
Northern Ireland, the target *is* police officers.[235]

Although Chief Constable Flanagan argued that officers "want to be a
community police force,"[236] Breidge Gadd, chief probation officer for Northern
Ireland, told Human Rights Watch/Helsinki that this will be difficult as long as the
RUC retains powers under the emergency legislation that create the very barriers
both Annesley and Flanagan have referred to:

> The main reason punishment beatings take place is that if you
> move a civilian police force into being the frontline fighters of
> terrorism,[237] and if that terrorism is endemic in certain
> communities as in Northern Ireland, it is obvious that you will
> lose the confidence of those communities in the civilian police

[235]This assertion is born out by a number of IRA-claimed attacks on police
officers, British soldiers, and RUC barracks since December 1996. Mortar bombs have been
fired at RUC land rover patrols and at police stations. In December 1996, IRA gunmen shot
and injured an RUC officer guarding Democratic Unionist Party politician Nigel Dodds on
a visit to his son at the Royal Victoria Hospital for Sick Children. See Robert Love,
"Memories of Darkest Hours of the Troubles Brought To Mind," *Irish News*, February 8,
1997. The IRA also claimed responsibility for a rocket attack on a security post manned by
an RUC officer at the Belfast High Court in January 1997. See James F. Clarity, "'Like the
Bad Old Days' as Fright Revisits Ulster," *New York Times*, January 13, 1997. An IRA
sniper shot and killed twenty-three-year-old British infantryman Stephen Restorick at a
checkpoint in the village of Bessbrook, thirty miles from Belfast, in February 1997. See
William D. Montalbano, "British Soldier's Death Comes After Accelerating Attacks," *Los
Angeles Times*, February 14, 1997. In April 1997, a part-time policewoman was injured
seriously when she was shot by an IRA sniper while on guard duty outside the
London/Derry Crown Court. See "More on Policewoman Shooting in Londonderry,"
London Press Association News, FBIS-TOT-97-100, April 10, 1997.

[236]Human Rights Watch/Helsinki interview, Belfast, November 24, 1996.

[237]In the mid-1970s, the government initiated the process of "Police Primacy."
The goal of this policy was to have the RUC assume overall responsibility for security
operations in Northern Ireland, displacing the primacy of the British army in security
matters. See Urban, *Big Boys' Rules*, p. 15.

force. You can't have both in one force. One day, the police are
kicking down your door, taking the house apart and treating you
like a terrorist. The next morning, you can't call the police to
report a burglary. Even though the RUC may be able to change
roles, the local community aren't as trusting nor is it that easy for
them to solve their ambivalences. Until there is resolution
between the police and those communities most affected by
crime and terrorism, there will continue to be punishment
beatings.[238]

William Smith of the Progressive Unionist Party (PUP) told us that there
is an added dimension to the abrogation of normal policing in unionist areas.
Smith claims that the class differences between RUC officers and residents of
working class unionist communities causes a lack of trust in the RUC.

What you have in the RUC in the past ten years is a class-based
force. After the Anglo-Irish Agreement, when all those
policemen's homes were attacked, they moved out to the
suburbs. Punishment beatings happened in the first place
because the police lost control of the neighborhoods and lived
outside of the communities. We had mobile support units and
land rovers and there was no attempt at policing as such. When
people phoned the police about burglaries or non-terrorist
crimes, they abdicated their responsibilities. There was an
abdication because the police retreated to land rovers and looked
for paramilitary activity. Paramilitaries filled the vacuum they
didn't want to fill. The police force is more tolerated, not more
welcome in loyalist areas.[239]

John Steele of the Northern Ireland Office (NIO) told us that "there is no
justification for these horrible attacks. They are grotesquely inhumane. And it
happens on both sides."[240] But when queried by Human Rights Watch/Helsinki

---

[238]Human Rights Watch/Helsinki interview, Belfast, November 18, 1996.

[239]Human Rights Watch/Helsinki interview, Belfast, November 22, 1996.

[240]Human Rights Watch/Helsinki interview, Belfast, November 12, 1996.

regarding the relationship between the police and paramilitary punishments, NIO official Christine Collins replied:

> What can the police do? What can the police do that is in any
> way as direct and satisfying as what the IRA does?[241]

This response suggests that the RUC is justified in abrogating its normal policing responsibilities because people want this type of summary justice and not because of legitimate security concerns related to possible terrorist activity.[242] Such an admission by a government official is particularly disturbing. The government cannot respond to the phenomenon of alternative "justice" systems by simply throwing its hands up in surrender. The Northern Ireland authorities have *de facto* delegated authority to the paramilitary groups in some areas and must be held accountable for relinquishing to them what is a primary responsibility of government—the duty to protect citizens from arbitrary acts of violence.

The police and paramilitary organizations must share responsibility for the existence of alternative "justice" systems. Paramilitary organizations bear responsibility for the infliction of physical and psychological harm that often amounts to torture on members of their own communities. The RUC and the government of the United Kingdom must be held accountable for relinquishing responsibility for normal policing to paramilitary organizations.

Human Rights Watch/Helsinki concludes that the government of the United Kingdom must assume responsibility for the immediate resumption of normal policing, that is, non-terrorist related policing, and the administration of

---

[241]Ibid.

[242]The claim that paramilitaries respond to community pressures to "do something" about crime in the neighborhoods is an attenuated one. Liam Kennedy notes that

> the elastic notion of "community" demand as the primary basis for primitive forms of vengeance and deterrence is essentially a smokescreen. Paramilitaries show scant regard for popular opinion, unless it serves their strategic interests. . .It would be more accurate to speak of *factional* rather than community support for the "rough justice" practised by the paramilitaries—an acquiescence in human rights violations to be found mainly but not exclusively among the minorities of unionists and nationalists who favour violence as a means of effecting political change.

Kennedy, "Nightmares within Nightmares," p. 76.

criminal justice in troubled areas. Likewise, it must provide adequate resources and protection for police officers to carry out such duties.

Role of the Paramilitaries

Parallel criminal justice systems are not a new phenomenon, particularly in the nationalist community.[243] It is not within the scope of this report to detail the historical development of such systems. The phenomenon of punishment shootings and beatings as discussed in this report, however, is a relatively recent form of paramilitary policing distinguished from prior incarnations by its summary procedures, harsh sentences, brutal execution of those sentences, frequency of attacks, and alleged community support.

Social workers, politicians, former paramilitaries, and victims offered many explanations for why paramilitary organizations would assume responsibility for policing the neighborhoods. Many asserted that residents in the neighborhoods pressured the paramilitary groups into assuming policing responsibilities. Alex Maskey, Sinn Féin spokesperson on policing, told Human Rights Watch/Helsinki:

> Ordinary communities and people want crime stopped. Going back fifteen years, Martin McGuinness gave an Easter oration and addressed the debate over punishments. He said the community needs to get involved in this. The IRA withdrew. Republicans tried to set up social and community groups but, at the end of the day, the cry went up to do something about crime.[244]

According to Chief Probation Officer Gadd, residents in nationalist communities do not view the RUC as a legitimate police force and pressure paramilitaries into assuming a policing role.

---

[243]See J.S. Donnelly, "The Whiteboy Movement, 1761-5," *Irish Historical Studies*, 21 (1978) and "The Terry Alt Movement, 1829-31" *History Ireland*, 2 (1994); Michael Morrissey and Ken Pease, "The Black Criminal Justice System in West Belfast," *The Howard Journal*, volume XXI, 1982; D. MacCardle, *The Irish Republic*, (Irish Press: Dublin, 1951), pp. 347-349; Ronnie Munck, "The Lads and the Hoods: Alternative Justice in the Irish Context," in M. Tomlinson, et. al., eds., *Whose Law & Order?* (Belfast, 1988).

[244]Human Rights Watch/Helsinki interview, Belfast, November 19, 1996.

After the cease-fire, there was an attempt by the republican movement to stop punishment beatings. Meetings were held where the local communities demanded the republican force to continue acting. These are not crazy men exerting control. If they stopped and there was no agreement with the state police force to come back and start policing, there would be anarchy.[245]

Mary Osborne, manager of the West Belfast Parent Youth Support Group on the Falls Road, agreed that there is community support for paramilitary punishments. She claimed that she has heard people say that the IRA "couldn't shoot enough of them or they [the IRA] should shoot them through the head."[246] One commentator wrote, "The community is terrorised by petty criminals: the community has a right to respond. What could be more logical, more democratic than that?"[247]

Working class Protestants respond to loyalist paramilitary policing in a strikingly similar fashion. A Protestant probation officer on the Shankill Road told Human Rights Watch/Helsinki that there is "no way" people in loyalist communities will go to the police and give their names because they are afraid they will be perceived as informers.[248] From her perspective, there is "no rhyme or reason" for the punishments but the "paramilitaries say that the community actually wants the beatings to happen. We have to encourage people to give information to the police instead of the paramilitaries."[249]

David Nichol, London/Derry-based representative for the Ulster Democratic Party (UDP), confirms that residents in working class loyalist communities have some of the same fears and suspicions about the RUC as do nationalists:

---

[245]Human Rights Watch/Helsinki interview, Belfast, November 18, 1996.

[246]Human Rights Watch/Helsinki interview, Belfast, November 21, 1996.

[247]B. Rolston, "Morality Play," *The Chartist*, 7 (1991). As cited in Kennedy, "Nightmares within Nightmares," p. 75.

[248]Human Rights Watch/Helsinki interview, Belfast, November 21, 1996.

[249]Ibid.

I can understand the frustration of the local populace. They
repeatedly call the RUC who refuse to act and use informers to
keep an eye on paramilitaries. The community itself won't
cooperate with the RUC to put people away because of the fear
which the populace has in the first place of coming to the
RUC.[250]

Many people do not believe that community pressure is the sole, or even
most significant, force at work in convincing paramilitaries to take up policing.
Human Rights Watch/Helsinki spoke with many members of both communities
who believe that paramilitary interests are paramount to any collective community
interests. Thomas Clarke, whose son Malachy committed suicide after being
victimized by an IRA punishment beating, is a volunteer with Families Against
Intimidation and Terror (FAIT), a support and advocacy group for victims of
paramilitary intimidation. Clarke claims:

The idea of Sinn Féin being community police is an absolute
sham. It has to do with one thing: controlling the areas through
the use of terror because the level of fear of the people in the
areas where paramilitary influence is the strongest is
unbelievable. People who support this type of policing are part
of the cancer. You have to break the power of the paramilitaries'
capacity to terrorize families.[251]

Jeff Maxwell, a crisis intervention worker with Base 2, an agency which
provides crisis support for persons under threat of paramilitary intimidation, told
Human Rights Watch/Helsinki that:

A lot of it's about the paramilitaries making themselves
indispensable within the community. Sex offenders is a popular
issue. In the past, Sinn Féin would go to another organization to
have the RUC called. Now, the paramilitaries are more

---

[250]Human Rights Watch/Helsinki interview, London/Derry, November 23, 1996.

[251]Human Rights Watch/Helsinki interview, Belfast, November 15, 1996.

successful at driving sex offenders out because it's very popular
with the local community.[252]

A representative of a large voluntary organization told us that another
explanation for the role of paramilitaries in policing communities has to do with the
brokered absence of paramilitary violence during the cease-fires. He commented
on the marked increase in punishment beatings and expulsions during the
paramilitary cease-fires and stated that meting out punishments was "a way of
keeping the volunteers[253] busy during the cease-fires and, with respect to the
policing debate, it kept the issue of policing at the forefront."[254] Alex Maskey
agreed that IRA volunteers carry out the punishments but added that the
"volunteers themselves are very critical of having to take that action. An IRA
volunteer doesn't see this kind of activity as their role."[255]

Liam Kennedy has written about the kinds of paramilitary interests
advanced by punishment shootings and beatings:

> First, in the context of a state whose legitimacy is contested, the
> will to supplant the police and the judicial system is part of a
> wider struggle to destroy British rule in Northern Ireland. This
> applies to republican paramilitaries but not of course to loyalists.
> Moreover, by cutting off more conventional policing alternatives
> in some neighbourhoods, paramilitaries can help manufacture
> "community" support for their punitive activities. Secondly,
> internal repression gives a degree of control, through terror or
> the threat of terror, over those who might be less than supportive
> of a particular paramilitary organization. Thirdly, in relation to
> those who are broadly supportive of political violence,
> "punishments" offer gratifying confirmation of the benefits of
> allegiance: fast retaliation in the face of any provocation,
> including criminal activity locally. Puritanical impulses to
> "clean-up" society, to rid an area of "anti-social" elements, can

---

[252]Human Rights Watch/Helsinki interview, Belfast, November 18, 1996.

[253]Members of paramilitary organizations often are referred to as "volunteers."

[254]Human Rights Watch/Helsinki interview, Belfast, November 14, 1996.

[255]Human Rights Watch/Helsinki interview, Belfast, November 19, 1996.

be realised, thereby strengthening the support base of paramilitary organizations. In certain circumstances, anxiety about a drugs epidemic for instance, "punishments" and expulsions can be a means of extending popular support for politico-paramilitary parties. Fourthly, "punishments" can be a means of disciplining rival groups . . . Or it can be a means of enforcing internal discipline, as would seem to be the case within the UDA in the late 1980s.[256]

A former loyalist paramilitary who was a victim of a UDA punishment shooting told Human Rights Watch/Helsinki that, in addition to "taking care of anti-social elements" within the loyalist community, punishments are used as a means of internal discipline.[257] He claimed that "you join one group and then leave under threat and then join another paramilitary group for protection."[258] A youth worker on the Shankill Road told us that threats of beatings are also being used by loyalist paramilitaries as a method of recruitment:

The stats in no way reflect the problem. A lot of work goes on behind the scenes. There is a spate of younger people being threatened to join paramilitary groups. Recruitment is going on at schools![259]

The prevalence of racketeering and drug trafficking arose many times in conversations about the role of paramilitaries in policing communities. Very few people were willing to go on record, or even discuss at any length, the fact that racketeering plays an important role in paramilitary repression. One man, a Protestant who had been the victim of a punishment beating, told Human Rights Watch/Helsinki that the punishment beatings in the loyalist community are "all about money. Extortion. Protection money. Nearly all the shops in west Belfast[260]

---

[256]Kennedy, "Nightmares within Nightmares," p. 77.

[257]Human Rights Watch/Helsinki interview, Belfast, November 21, 1996.

[258]Ibid.

[259]Human Rights Watch/Helsinki interview, Belfast, November 21, 1996.

[260]This man was referring to shops on the Protestant Shankill Road.

pay protection money."[261] A youth worker on the Shankill Road told the mission that "the depth of the drug problem is great and increasing rapidly. One of the main loyalist paramilitary activities is dealing drugs."[262] A probation officer, also working in a loyalist area, told us that "the paramilitaries have to survive. Once there was a cease-fire, 'fines' have come into force. It is really protection money."[263]

Jeff Maxwell of Base 2 explained how racketeering occurs in some loyalist communities:

> In loyalist areas, you take a loan from someone who is a member of a paramilitary organization. They are running the local shebeens [drinking clubs]. Social clubs, taxi drivers, and shops pay protection money. The depot pays the paramilitaries seven pounds per taxi on the road per week. It is organized crime. The loyalist side is directly involved in selling drugs. Both sides take cuts from people who operate in their areas.[264]

Base 2 reported thirty-seven referrals for punishment beatings by loyalist paramilitaries in January 1997 alone.[265] By contrast, in 1994 there were thirty-eight loyalist punishment beatings in the entire year. A crisis intervention worker told Human Rights Watch/Helsinki that this shocking increase in loyalist punishment attacks is a result of internal rivalries between the UDA and the UVF related to loyalist drug dealing in Portadown.[266]

---

[261]Human Rights Watch/Helsinki interview, Belfast, November 21, 1996.

[262]Human Rights Watch/Helsinki interview, Belfast, November 21, 1996.

[263]Human Rights Watch/Helsinki interview, Belfast, November 21, 1996.

[264]Human Rights Watch/Helsinki interview, Belfast, November 18, 1996.

[265]Human Rights Watch/Helsinki telephone interview, January 1997.

[266]Human Rights Watch/Helsinki telephone interview, February 19, 1997.

The Victims of Punishments

According to RUC statistics, from 1982 through 1996 there were 1,129 punishment assaults.[267] Roughly 60 percent of these assaults are attributed to republican paramilitaries and 40 percent are attributed to loyalist paramilitaries. In 1994, prior to the cease-fires, the RUC reported thirty-eight assaults by loyalist groups and thirty-two by republican groups. The 1995 statistics indicate a disturbing increase in punishments with loyalist assaults doubling to seventy-six and republican assaults more than quadrupling to 141. The overall number of punishment assaults nearly tripled from seventy-six in 1994 to 217 in 1995. The worst year in the history of Northern Ireland for reported punishment assaults was 1996 with 172 attributed to republican groups and 130 attributed to loyalist groups.

From 1990 through 1996, punishment shootings attributed to loyalist paramilitary groups consistently outnumbered those attributed to republican paramilitaries. The overall number of punishment shootings decreased dramatically from 1994 to 1995. This can be explained by the cease-fire agreements entered into by all paramilitary groups in late 1994. There were sixty-eight punishment shootings by loyalists and fifty-four by republicans in 1994. In 1995, no punishment shootings were attributed to republicans and three were attributed to loyalists.[268] In 1996, there were three punishment shootings by republican paramilitaries and twenty-four by loyalist paramilitaries.

In addition to an increase in punishment assaults during the cease-fires, Jeff Maxwell of Base 2 told Human Rights Watch/Helsinki that there are a number of recent developments with respect to punishments:

---

[267]RUC, "Casualties as a Result of Punishment Assaults 1982-1996 (31 August)," November 1996. Figures for September 1-December 31, 1996 are contained in Table 14, "Casualties as a Result of Paramilitary Style Attacks Broken Down by Loyalist and Republican Groups 1991-1996," in Letter from RUC Chief Constable Ronnie Flanagan to Human Rights Watch/Helsinki, March 7, 1997. All figures below are derived from these two RUC sources.

[268]The RUC did not include eight killings committed in 1995-1996, claimed by Direct Action Against Drugs (DAAD), in its punishment shootings statistical report despite the fact that then RUC Chief Constable Hugh Annesley had "no doubt whatsoever" that the IRA was responsible for the DAAD murders. Gerry Moriarty, "RUC Says Recent Murders in North Sanctioned at Highest Level of IRA," *Irish Times*, January 6, 1996. There has been speculation that the RUC quietly avoided officially labeling these killings as republican paramilitary punishment shootings for fear that the cease-fires would be threatened. (See section below titled "Direct Action Against Drugs: Summary Executions of Alleged Drug Dealers.")

There has been an increase in the number of under sixteen-year-olds being told to leave an area. We have some thirteen-year-olds. There's also been an increase in the number of women who've been threatened. In 1995, it was only 1 to 2 percent. For July/August/September of 1996, it's 15 percent. There has been a rise in the number of women dealing drugs. In the absence of shootings, there is an increase in expulsions and a step-up in enforcement. There's a notable increase in paramilitaries going back and checking to see if they've actually gone and aren't just out of sight. Because of more vigorous enforcement, a lot more people are afraid they'll be caught.

There 's been an increase in severity. People have been beaten with baseball bats with spikes in them. People have been hung over railings. Since the cease-fire, there's been a big increase in the severity of beatings on the republican side. No shootings so much as atrocious beatings. Ask any young person, they'd much rather be shot. They're told to lie on the ground and they're shot. A beating can last ten to fifteen minutes. Shooting takes a minute and the ambulance is called. Or ask someone who's had both and they'll tell you they'd rather be shot. Some people had been shot three or four times, healed, and were out again offending so the IRA tried to do greater damage. They shot them through the back of the knee, the popliteal artery. If untreated, there is reduced blood flow and this can cause amputations. A number of people have had limbs amputated. The IRA and UDA are using active service units to do it. They are taking to it with greater gusto than normal.[269]

The RUC, Base 2 and FAIT all caution that the statistics they record do not reflect the depth of the problem presented by punishments. Many attacks go unreported due to fear of further intimidation by paramilitaries who threaten victims with retaliation if they report to the police. Sam Cushnahan, a representative of FAIT, told Human Rights Watch/Helsinki:

Up until two years ago, there was no problem getting people to come to FAIT. The paramilitaries came under so much pressure

---

[269]Human Rights Watch/Helsinki interview, Belfast, November 18, 1996.

from everyone, including the Americans, so it embarrassed the paramilitaries. Now, they warn people, "we know you and if we can't get you, we'll get a member of your family and we'll do the same thing to them that we've done to you."[270]

Direct Action Against Drugs (DAAD): Summary Executions of Alleged Drug Dealers

From April 1995 through September 1996 eight men were shot dead in Belfast and Lurgan in the name of a group called Direct Action Against Drugs (DAAD). Obliged to halt all forms of violence by the cease-fire agreement it entered into in August 1994, the IRA is widely believed to have used DAAD as a cover organization to carry out killings of alleged drug traffickers. Sinn Féin, the political arm of the IRA, refused to condemn the killings leading to further speculation that the IRA was behind the murders. Shortly after one of the killings, Sinn Féin councillor Michael Ferguson refused nine times to condemn the murder, stating only that Sinn Féin did not condone it.[271] Speculation appeared at an end in January 1996 after a Sinn Féin delegation met with Irish government officials and Pat Doherty, Sinn Féin vice-president, said that Sinn Féin was trying to halt the killings; a posture that was widely read as an acknowledgment that the IRA was responsible.[272] The eight men murdered were:

* Mickey "Moneybags" Mooney, April 28, 1995, Belfast
* Tony Kane, September 9, 1995, Belfast
* Paul "Saul" Devine, December 8, 1995, Belfast
* Francis "Fra" Collins, December 18, 1995, Belfast
* Christopher "Sid" Johnston, December 19, 1995, Belfast
* Martin McCrory, December 27, 1995, Belfast
* Ian Lyons, January 1, 1996, Lurgan
* Sean Devlin, September 16, 1996, Belfast

---

[270]Human Rights Watch/Helsinki interview, Belfast, November 15, 1996.

[271]David Sharrock, "Peace Fails to Stop Bloody IRA Justice," *The Guardian*, December 12, 1995.

[272]David Sharrock, "U.S. Envoy's Return Could Halt Wave of IRA Killings," *The Guardian*, January 8, 1996.

The RUC was accused of having approached the subject of the killings "with diplomatic caution" at first in order to hold together the fragile cease-fire.[273] After five men were murdered in as many weeks, the RUC firmly pinned responsibility for the murders on the IRA and created a special team to investigate the killings.[274]

Press accounts claimed the killings were a response to "a policing vacuum in strongholds where many Catholics mistrust the largely Protestant police force and fear a 'flood of drugs' ruining their lives."[275] Some commentators asserted that the killings were a show of strength by the IRA at a time when the decommissioning of paramilitary weapons was the principle issue stalling the peace negotiations.[276]

Anne Collins, the widow of Francis "Fra" Collins, told Human Rights Watch/Helsinki that her husband, a former leader of the IRA in north Belfast and former republican prisoner, was not involved with drugs and that the killing occurred because of a personal vendetta.[277] Fra Collins was reportedly well known within the republican movement for his expertise at bank robberies, and, according to his widow, he committed a number of robberies to raise funds for IRA coffers. In 1989, after he had left the IRA, Fra Collins apparently committed a robbery for his own enrichment. He was sentenced to seven years in prison for the robbery and was released in July 1994. According to Anne Collins, there was resentment within the republican movement after Fra committed the robbery "because a person of Fra's standing shouldn't have done it for himself."[278]

---

[273]Dick Walsh, "Murders May be a Signal of Strength," *Irish Times*, January 6, 1996.

[274]Chris Hagan, "RUC Reject 'Fudge' on Drug Deaths," *Irish News*, January 8, 1996.

[275]Martin Cowley, "Shadow of the Gunman Returns to Belfast," *Reuters*, January 9, 1996.

[276]Walsh, "Murders May be a Signal of Strength." Walsh asks, "Are the murders meant to illustrate how, after a cease fire lasting 16 months, SF/IRA is still a coherent force, with both wings in tact, united and responsive to clear commands?"

[277]Human Rights Watch/Helsinki interview, Belfast, November 15, 1996.

[278]Ibid.

Anne Collins described to us how she and her husband came to learn of allegations of drug involvement from some of Fra Collins' friends in the republican movement. Fra Collins sought help from a Sinn Féin councillor[279] to clear his name.[280]

> Fra asked [the councillor] to go over to the Falls Road and to help get his name cleared. [The councillor] rang two days later, this is in September of 1995, and said there would be two men over to see Fra in the next two weeks. The meeting would give Fra a chance to tell his side and then the thing was pretty much wrapped up. No one came in the next two weeks. On December 7, our chip shop opened. We put everything into it. There was still no word from [the councillor]. We're a republican family and we know the workings. Since no one came back to us, no news is good news.[281]

John Hunter, Anne's brother and a former IRA member, told Human Rights Watch/Helsinki that, after no one came to meet with Fra, they thought it was taken care of.[282] Anne Collins, who was in the chip shop working with Fra the night he was killed, told us that on December 18, 1995:

> Fra came into the chip shop after 5:00 p.m. He did the potatoes in the back. Afterward, I made him something to eat. Fra sat down to eat. He got up and went through the door to the back of the kitchen. When he was coming back, he said "Hey, Anne!" and then I heard the four shots. I thought it was bangers [fireworks]. At first, I put my head down and then I realized that it was shooting. I jumped up and ran round the side of the

---

[279]The name of the councillor is withheld for security reasons.

[280]A determination of whether or not Francis Collins was involved in drugs is beyond the mandate of Human Rights Watch/Helsinki. Both Anne and Fra Collins maintained that Fra was not involved in drugs. Moreover, summary execution under any circumstances is a violation of the right to life.

[281]Human Rights Watch/Helsinki interview, Belfast, November 15, 1996.

[282]Human Rights Watch/Helsinki interview, Belfast, November 15, 1996.

counter where Fra was. I saw two men with their backs to me; only three feet away from me. They ran out and I run out after them. I shouted "Youse bastards!" and they shouted "Up the 'Ra!"[283]

I came back inside the shop and knelt down beside him. I couldn't see no blood at first. I ran down to phone...999 for emergency. I gave the operator the details. He was still breathing but turning gray. His eyes were open but he didn't speak to me. Some people took me out of the shop. The ambulance came and took him to hospital. The person who lives opposite the shop took me to hospital. They brought me into a wee, private room. Ten minutes later a nurse came in and told me the news wasn't good. I asked her had Fra died and she said "yes."[284]

John Hunter told Human Rights Watch/Helsinki that he thought it was loyalist paramilitaries.

We assumed it was loyalists until the next morning. Fra was shot on December 18. On December 19, Sid Johnston was shot dead. That was the first time "DAAD" was used. They put posters up in this area with the names of people who were drug dealers. Anyone suspected of drug dealing, name on a poster and let your name be known. But Fra's name never appeared and no one ever came here. No death threats, no warnings.[285]

The IRA did not claim responsibility for the murder of Fra Collins or for any of the DAAD killings.[286] However, Alex Maskey, Sinn Féin spokesperson on policing, acknowledged that punishments can be the mode for settling old scores:

---

[283]IRA.

[284]Human Rights Watch/Helsinki interview, Belfast, November 15, 1996.

[285]Human Rights Watch/Helsinki interview, Belfast, November 15, 1996.

[286]Gerry Moriarty, "RUC says Recent Murders in North Sanctioned at Highest Level of IRA," *Irish Times*, January 6, 1996.

This is a huge human rights dilemma for me and my party. There are human rights violations involved. This can be a very crude form of justice dispensation. The reasons? Retribution, deterrence, revenge. People say there are no police to go to. Major demands are made on republicans to handle crime problems, especially drugs. People think we could be heading for a Dublin situation. People are terrified by that. Naturally, people will go to the IRA and ask them to do something about it. Punishments have been very popular but sometimes these things amount to revenge.[287]

Seamus Mallon, SDLP deputy leader claimed in January 1996 that "the IRA has called off its murder campaign against alleged drug dealers."[288] Mallon said:

The killings were a spurious imposition of the IRA's will on the community. It was a test of strength of its organization. It is something which I now believe has stopped.[289]

Despite Mallon's assurances, Sean Devlin was killed by gunmen acting in the name of DAAD in September 1996. There have been no murders claimed on behalf of DAAD since then. There have also been no convictions to date for these murders. Human Rights Watch/Helsinki condemns these killings in the strongest possible terms and calls on the perpetrators to halt these unjust and inhumane attacks.

---

[287]Human Rights Watch/Helsinki interview, Belfast, November 19, 1996. In June 1996, Veronica Guerin was the first journalist in the Republic of Ireland to be killed for exposing criminal activities related to drug-trafficking. The rising drug problem in the Republic has been the subject of much public debate and has led to calls for harsher criminal sanctions for suspected drug traffickers. See Michael McCaughan, "Could Ireland Go the Way of the Colombians?" *Irish Times*, June 29, 1996.

[288]Rory Carroll, "Drug Deaths are Over says Mallon," *Irish News*, January 20, 1996.

[289]Ibid.

The Ulster Defense Association (UDA): Punishment Shootings

Human Rights Watch/Helsinki was unable to interview the UDA about punishment shootings and assaults, and attitudes toward policing. The mission met with unionist politicians, former UDA paramilitaries, and victims of punishment shootings to discuss paramilitary repression in loyalist areas.

As noted above, loyalist paramilitaries "police" their communities for "anti-social" behavior. They also mete out punishments as a means of internal discipline or as a means of recruitment to their organizations. Prior to the cease-fires, both the IRA and UDA favored punishment shootings over punishment beatings. These shootings, commonly referred to as "kneecappings," involved shots to the knee joints resulting in damage to the kneecaps, soft tissue, tendons, muscles, arteries and veins, and nerve damage. In some instances, paramilitaries gave a punishment victim a "six pack": shots to the ankles, the knees, and the elbows or wrists.

A former UDA paramilitary on the Shankill Road told Human Rights Watch/Helsinki that he had been a victim of a punishment shooting:

> I was shot by the UDA for being in a row. No questions asked.
> They came to my house and told me where to be. I knew I was
> going to get shot.[290]

This former paramilitary did not consider the call at his house as a warning. It was merely a chance for the paramilitaries to give instructions regarding where to be and at what time. One community worker who spoke with Helsinki Watch in 1992, reported that "Generally, republicans give advance warnings before punishment shootings or assaults, but loyalists don't ."[291]

Kenneth Bankhead, a twenty-six year old Protestant, was shot by loyalist paramilitaries in August 1996. According to Bankhead, he was not a member of a loyalist paramilitary group. On the evening of August 8, 1996, he drove from his girlfriend's house in Highfield to his home in Rathcoole, a loyalist stronghold, about nine miles outside Belfast.

> I got out of my car and went to open the garage door. Three
> hooded men came round at me from about fifteen meters away.
> I tried to run but I saw a gun aiming low toward my legs before

---

[290]Human Rights Watch/Helsinki interview, Belfast, November 21, 1996.

[291]See Human Rights Watch/Helsinki, *Children in Northern Ireland*, p. 43.

I turned. As I was turning, there was a shot in my leg just above the left knee. I still managed to run believe it or not. I was hopping and skipping. Then they fired again from about three foot away and missed. Just after the second bullet, I was still running at the time, I didn't hear no footsteps behind me. I turned and saw the three of them running up the back fields. I hobbled to the front of the road and collapsed. I was in the hospital for two and a half weeks. I had a bullet wound to the left leg. The bullet busted the artery so they had to take artery from my right leg and put it into my left leg. The next day in the hospital my family told me the UDA did it. They branded me a police informer.[292]

Bankhead reported that he had been threatened with a beating by a leading UDA man who had a grudge against him from their football-playing days. In addition, he had been interrogated by a UDA council which included this same man:

Three to four weeks before I was shot, the UDA were rioting in Rathcoole, burning out buses. I was driving home to my flat during the riot and three UDA men tried to hijack my motor [car]. I saw them coming at me with the hoods on and I reversed and almost hit them. I just sped away. I had to go over a field to get away from them. A few days later, I was pulled into a UDA interrogation. They threatened to shoot me because I near hit two of their members. There were seven of them. The two at the door were hooded and five weren't. They were a UDA brigade staff. They threatened me that they were gonna shoot me, break my arms, break my legs. The head guy told me I'd never play football again. They let me go but he said, "I guarantee you, you'll not play football again." Three weeks later I was shot. They tried to justify it by saying I was a police informer.[293]

Bankhead said there is an extremely high level of paramilitary repression in Rathcoole. He claimed that "young kids can barely breathe. There's beatings,

---

[292]Human Rights Watch/Helsinki interview, Belfast, November 20, 1996.

[293]Human Rights Watch/Helsinki interview, Belfast, November 20, 1996.

shootings, people getting arms and legs broken." He noted that this type of activity is "common in most Protestant neighborhoods" but not to the extent that it is in Rathcoole. When asked whether he reported the shooting to the police, Bankhead told us that although he knew who shot him, he didn't name him because "it's like taking on the mafia if you do that. I told the police that there were three hooded men and I didn't get a good description of them. They were masked, so they'll not be caught."[294]

According to Bankhead, there is an internal procedure for redressing his grievances: a meeting with the entire UDA Council throughout Belfast:

> I been trying since I got out of the hospital. I'm going through top men up the Shankill, everywhere, to get my name cleared. The meeting means I go before the UDA Council, the top ten men, and put my case forward against this man. He'll have his case, too. He can't just go around shooting people. He's got to have evidence that I'm a police informer. It's not a very nice label to be tagged with. I don't think I could ever feel safe again. I barely go out at night time now. Getting branded a police informer isn't very nice because police informers are taken away and shot in the head. In the UDA areas, that's the way it works.[295]

FAIT records a decrease in punishment shootings overall but reports that they still occur despite the continuing Combined Loyalist Military Command (CLMC) cease-fire.[296] On February 3, 1997, FAIT reported that a twenty-four-year-old Protestant man was assaulted by a gang of masked men between Rathcoole and Whitehouse. He was shot and suffered serious injuries to his right leg.

The UDA: Punishment Assaults

According to statistics from the Tennent Street RUC station, the official number of reported punishment beatings in the loyalist Greater Shankill area in 1995 was ten. In the first four months of 1996, the number of loyalist punishment

---

[294]Ibid.

[295]Ibid.

[296]See the Introduction to this report for a description of the tenuous state of the CLMC cease fire.

assaults in the Greater Shankill was fourteen. It is undisputed that these are historically high levels of assault.

In 1992, Raymond McCord, then thirty-eight years old, alleged that he was brutally beaten by the UDA. McCord had both legs and arms broken, a broken nose, and cracked ribs. He told Human Rights Watch/Helsinki:

> The UDA rules by terror in Protestant areas. I refused to join them when I was seventeen, and over the years they decided to make me an example. . .The beating they gave me in February was the worst beating in my area in twenty years. I've charged them with my beating—I'm the first person in twenty years to do that. They attacked me outside a bar with flagstones. They dropped flagstones on my arms and legs and kicked my face while I was lying on the ground. Their usual weapons are baseball bats.[297]

In September 1996, loyalist paramilitaries were held responsible by the authorities for two attacks on the homes of Protestant families in Belfast. *The Irish Times* reported that one of the homes was attacked because the man who lived there had two brothers, both of whom "fell out" with the UDA in early 1996 and were forced to leave Northern Ireland.[298]

In early 1997, FAIT reported the following loyalist paramilitary punishment attacks:

- On January 27, 1997, a nineteen-year-old man was abducted from his home in the Rathcoole area by five masked men wielding clubs and a gun. The man was brought to an area close to Rathfern. He received a broken leg, a broken ankle and bruises to the face and body.

- On February 7, 1997, a forty-two-year-old man was assaulted at his home in Ballyduff, Newtownabbey. Three masked men beat him with cudgels spiked with nails resulting in two broken legs with puncture wounds and a suspected fractured skull. The man subsequently died.

---

[297]Human Rights Watch/Helsinki, *Children in Northern Ireland*, pp. 43-44.

[298]Carol Coulter, "Loyalists Blamed for Two Belfast Attacks," *Irish Times*, September 9, 1996.

Despite strong evidence of the persistence of punishment attacks in the loyalist community, Jeffrey Donaldson, honorary secretary of the Ulster Unionist Party (UUP), told Human Rights Watch/Helsinki:

> There is not sufficient support in the loyalist community to support the current level of violence by loyalist paramilitaries. Loyalist paramilitaries signed onto Mitchell thus loyalist punishment beatings have virtually ended. Now, there are substantial fines. There is still violence but it is mainly drug-related. The Unionist Party stood out against any efforts by loyalists to impose control on the loyalist community. We've had a substantial impact on controlling the type of severe policing activity in nationalist areas.[299]

Neither the statistics nor the testimony Human Rights Watch/Helsinki gathered during its mission bear out Donaldson's claims. Loyalist paramilitary repression remains a significant problem in loyalist communities. According to a study undertaken by Tom Winstone, a consultant for the Progressive Unionist Party (PUP), paramilitary punishment assaults in loyalist areas in the first quarter of 1996 exceeded the total number of assaults for 1995. Moreover, the results of a survey on policing in loyalist communities conducted by Winstone concluded:

> Many people felt that paramilitary punishment beating was not the ideal, but felt that at present it served as the only form of response that the community felt it had in dealing with the ever increasing crime rate. There was a general feeling that the community lacks respect for the police's ability to deal with those involved in anti-social behavior, leaving them no alternative but to approach paramilitaries.[300]

---

[299]Human Rights Watch/Helsinki interview, Belfast, November 20, 1996.

[300]Tom Winstone, *Initial Report into Crime Prevention in the Local Community*, commissioned by the Advisory Committee of the Progressive Unionist Party, Belfast, 1996, p. 8.

In some areas, however, loyalist paramilitaries appear to have adopted the idea of imposing fines on some petty criminals, drug pushers and other anti-social elements in so-called "kangaroo courts."[301] According to one press account:

> Penalties of up to £1,000 are being offered to criminals who want to avoid brutal punishment beatings, according to reports reaching the police. Police have identified a pub in the Shankill area where they believe leading paramilitary figures levy fines for men and teenagers identified as drug pushers, burglars or thieves.[302]

Human Rights Watch/Helsinki has no way of corroborating this account. None of the loyalists interviewed for this report mentioned a system of fines for "anti-social" behavior.

The Irish Republican Army (IRA): Punishment Shootings and Assaults

Mary Osborne, manager of the West Belfast Parent Youth Support Group on the Falls Road, told Human Rights Watch/Helsinki that there are internal procedures governing the use of punishments by the IRA:

> When young people come under warnings, they would come here. Certain members of the management would liaise with the paramilitaries. They'd try to define the threat. Usually it's because of joyriding or something like that. People in the areas where we come from don't go to the police because they know the police won't do anything. They would go to a Sinn Féin centre and it would be investigated. Nine times out of ten, there's a core element terrorizing the people and the police'll do nothing.[303]

In 1992, Joe Austin, a Sinn Féin councillor who represents a North Belfast district, explained to Human Rights Watch/Helsinki the mechanisms at work in the

---

[301]Alan Murray, "Loyalists Offering 'Beatings or Fines' at Kangaroo Courts," *Sunday Independent*, September 29, 1996.

[302]Ibid.

[303]Human Rights Watch/Helsinki interview, November 21, 1996.

republican parallel justice system. He claimed that civilian administrative panels, comprised solely of republicans whose only responsibility is to administer these cases, hear complaints from community members about criminal activity. The panels hear testimony and complainants, and those defending against the complaint, can bring witnesses to the panel. The panel then makes a decision to impose a fine or level a warning:

> For instance, if a seventeen-year-old is accused of housebreaking—breaking and entering—and there's proof of it, the parents will be visited by the IRA. They'll give the evidence to the parents, and advise the parents that their son is involved with bad company, or is drinking, or is a substance abuser, and tell the parents that they should keep an eye on the boy. If there is a second incident with the boy, the IRA will visit the parents again, and the boy will be curfewed—he might have to be home by 10:00 p.m. every night for about three months. If it's drink-related, he won't be allowed to be served in local pubs; all the pubs will be visited and told not to serve him. In 99.9 percent of the cases, the first visit is enough. In most of the cases, the second visit is enough. But if there's another recurrence, the boy will usually be physically punished.[304]

Austin claimed that "the last punishment option . . . is physical punishment or expulsion."[305] Alex Maskey, Sinn Féin spokesperson on policing, told Human Rights Watch/Helsinki in November 1996:

> Punishments are the last resort engaged in with respect to individuals. I would not be happy at all if it weren't the last resort. I don't want it to happen at all. It offends, it hurts, and it is politically disastrous.[306]

Despite claims of some rudimentary form of due process, Human Rights Watch/Helsinki spoke with many victims of punishments and their families who

[304]See Human Rights Watch/Helsinki, *Children in Northern Ireland*, p. 40.

[305]Ibid., p. 42.

[306]Human Rights Watch/Helsinki interview, November 19, 1996.

were never given a warning or a chance to appear before a panel before physical punishment was inflicted. Josie Ferris, a founder of the West Belfast Parent Youth Support Group and mother of nine children, recalls how her seventeen-year-old son was a victim of a punishment shooting in 1987 while playing table tennis at the youth drop in center:

> Neighbors came to me and said, "Declan's been shot." Usually they would warn you, but I never got told. They came in and ordered the kids to lay on the floor. There were five shootings the week Declan was shot. Six masked men came in. They were looking for five or six of them. They shot him in both legs. He never played football again. Usually they would come to the house and say "if he doesn't behave. . ." You'd get a second chance maybe the first time. At one time, I had fifteen on a football team and all of them had been shot.[307]

Human Rights Watch/Helsinki visited a Probation Day Centre in Belfast and met with a group of persistent, high-risk male offenders participating in the court-mandated Stop Think and Change (STAC) program. There were four men in their twenties, three Catholics and one Protestant. The Protestant man was the only one who had not been the victim of a punishment beating. Dominic, a Catholic from the New Lodge area of Belfast, recalled the punishment beating he received in 1990, when he was a teenager:

> I was walking down the street and got pulled into a car. They took me to Artillery Flats. There were five people, all wearing scarves. One said,"You know what you're getting this for!" They beat me with iron bars. I was beat unconscious. I woke up in hospital. I knew it was the IRA from the time it happened. It is too common. They do it to you for stealing cars, drug dealing, anything they deem it to be. But they seem to be getting younger and the beatings more severe. No use going to them because you'll only get some feeble excuse. The area I'm living in, it happens every day. You've got no choice. Don't have the finances to move. They see it as an alternative but the IRA is judge, jury and executioner. You don't get no say. They never went to my family once. The police can't stop this. I know three

---

[307]Human Rights Watch/Helsinki interview, Belfast, November 21, 1996.

of the people who did this to me but am I going to tell them? I
did anti-social behavior, yes. But what gives them the right?[308]

Thomas Clarke, a volunteer with FAIT, told Human Rights
Watch/Helsinki about his son, Malachy, who committed suicide after a republican
paramilitary punishment beating. Six months prior to the beating, a republican
paramilitary brought Malachy home after the boy had been sniffing glue. Malachy,
then sixteen years old, entered a treatment program and temporarily stopped
sniffing glue. In October 1994, Malachy had a relapse.

> Malachy was outside a shop with two friends having a can of
> beer. A car pulled up at the shop with two or three IRA men in
> it. They lived in the area. Everyone knew their names. Malachy
> had a bag of glue in his pocket. One of the IRA men went into
> the shop. When he came out, the driver drew his attention to
> Malachy's glue. One went over to my son and started to
> manhandle him, tried to take the glue off him. Malachy resisted
> and another man jumped out of the car and they tried to pull him
> around to a back alley. My son broke away and made it to an
> adjacent field. The IRA men went to a bar on the Falls Road and
> recruited another two or three men and they drove to the field
> and literally ambushed Malachy. They came at him from two
> sides. They gave him a beating, punched and kicked him for a
> few minutes and warned him never to use glue again. It seemed
> it was over when one of the lookout men came back and
> proceeded to start beating him all over again. So they beat him
> unconscious and poured the glue all over his head and face. He
> had a broken nose, two black eyes.[309]

Thomas Clarke interviewed several witnesses to the beating himself,
including one of Malachy's cousins who was with the boy the night he was beaten.
Clarke and Malachy eventually reported the beating to the police.

> The police made inquiries and contacted witnesses but no one
> was prepared to name names. They admitted there was an attack

---

[308]Human Rights Watch/Helsinki interview, November 21, 1996.

[309]Human Rights Watch/Helsinki interview, November 15, 1996.

but said they didn't know anything. During this time, Malachy
was frightened. When he goes out, they shout out of the
windows of their cars at him. They were intimidating him a lot.
So, he starts to stay at home and not go out. This goes on for six
or seven weeks. Everything's very tense. Six or seven weeks
after the attack, my son hanged himself in our home. I found my
son and he left a note: "Do not feel it is your fault as it is not. It
is the dirty, stinking piggy rats out on the street."[310]

Reports of brutal punishment beatings by republican paramilitaries are a
daily feature in newspapers. In June 1996, a twenty-one-year-old man was found
hanging upside down from railings in West Belfast. He was attacked by a number
of men who beat him with wooden clubs spiked with nails and iron bars.[311]
Twenty-four hours earlier, a sixteen-year-old was reported taken from his New
Barnsley home, tied upside down and beaten with spiked clubs.[312] The following
is a sample of reported attacks:

- Martin Doherty, age eighteen, from West Belfast, had metal spikes driven
  through his legs and elbows during a punishment attack on March 27,
  1996.[313] His mouth was taped and his hands were tied with plastic
  cuffs.[314]

- James Clarke, age twenty-two, was attacked outside an Ardoyne social
  club in February 1996. He was forced into a car, taken to an alleyway, and
  beaten with iron bars and hurley sticks. He suffered serious leg and head

---

[310]Ibid.

[311]Michael O'Toole, "RUC Lash 'Barbaric' Upside Down Beatings," *Irish News*,
June 28, 1996.

[312]Ibid.

[313]Gerry Moriarty, "SF/IRA Blamed by RUC for Vicious Beating," *Irish Times*,
March 28, 1996.

[314]David Sharrock, "Youth's Limbs Spiked in IRA Punishment Beating,"
Guardian, March 28, 1996.

injuries. He had been shot in both legs after a paramilitary punishment shooting four years earlier.[315]

- Denise Clarke, age sixteen, was dragged from her home in Twinbrook in October 1995 by a gang of men wearing scarves who tied her to a lamppost, cut her hair and poured paint over her.[316]

- Patrick Teer, age nineteen, was abducted from his home in North Belfast in February 1995, blindfolded for twenty-four hours, and severely beaten by a gang of men. His legs were pushed through the pickets of a wrought iron fence to immobilize them and his limbs were battered with steel pipes.[317]

Human Rights Watch/Helsinki asked Alex Maskey, Sinn Féin spokesperson on policing, whether the IRA planned to stop punishment attacks. Maskey responded, that "the IRA will not take the decision to stop them at this time."[318]

Expulsions

Both the IRA and the UDA issue expulsion orders directing people to leave a particular city or town, or all of Northern Ireland, under threat of being shot or beaten. Prior to the paramilitary cease-fires, shooting was the favored method of punishment. During the cease-fires, the number of reported expulsions increased dramatically and, as noted above, the degree of paramilitary enforcement of these expulsions increased. Base 2 reports that from January to December 1995, 131 clients were forced to leave their homes under threat of paramilitary

---

[315]Colin Carroll, "IRA Blamed by Mother after Gang Attacks Son," *Irish News*, February 27, 1996.

[316]Gerry Moriarty, "Violence and Terror Occur Almost Daily in the North Despite the Cease Fires," *Irish Times*, November 19, 1995.

[317]Barry Hillenbrand, "Afterlife of Violence," *Time*, June 12, 1995.

[318]Human Rights Watch/Helsinki interview, Belfast, November 19, 1996.

violence.[319] The 131 person total was an increase of forty-one compared to the number of 1994 expulsions. Base 2 stated that this increase "is probably related to a 'hardening' of attitudes by both republican and loyalist groups since the cease fires. Both are eager to use the policing issue for their own agendas."[320] From January to December 1996, Base 2 reported that 232 persons were forced to leave either their homes, cities, or Northern Ireland completely upon the issuance of an expulsion order by a paramilitary organization.[321] Individuals are not the only ones affected by paramilitary intimidation. Fifty-two of the 232 individuals expelled were forced to take their families with them resulting in the removal of 121 children from their homes and schools.[322]

According to Base 2, crisis intervention involves an attempt to intervene on behalf of individuals facing paramilitary threats by trying to maintain people in their homes. However, crisis intervention in the social work tradition does not easily adapt to paramilitary-style justice and is often unsuccessful:

> Should an individual be unable to be maintained in their own community, Base 2 would support attempts to place people with relatives. However, some people have no option but to leave Northern Ireland. Base 2 would then attempt to locate good quality placements outside of Northern Ireland. These placements would range from hostel accommodation through to the placement "package." This package would include the provision of accommodation, confrontation of behaviour, training, and, hopefully, a more settled and constructive lifestyle.[323]

---

[319]Of the total of 131 persons, fifty or 22.32 percent left their home address, twenty-six or 11.61 percent left the city in which they resided, and fifty-five or 24.54 percent left the country. See Table 1.11 "Client Action," *Base 2 Statistical Casework Overview: 1995*, p. 8.

[320]Ibid.

[321]NIACRO, *Overview of Casework Undertaken by Base 2 in 1996*, p. 9.

[322]Ibid., p. 10. Base 2 labels the families and children of those expelled the "hidden victims of paramilitary policing."

[323]*Base 2 Statistical Casework Overview: 1995*, p. 1

In our 1992 report *Children in Northern Ireland: Abused by the Security Forces and Paramilitaries*, Human Rights Watch/Helsinki recognized that one of the most disturbing results of RUC abdication of normal policing and resultant paramilitary "policing" was that social services agencies, crisis intervention counselors, and youth workers were "forced to choose between watching children be shot or viciously beaten by paramilitaries or helping paramilitaries to exile children."[324]

The Victims of Expulsions

Although there has been an increase in the number of expulsions since late 1994, the variety of ways by which a person learns of an expulsion order under paramilitary threat has remained relatively constant. A representative of a large voluntary organization told Human Rights Watch/Helsinki that expulsions in the nationalist community are highly organized:

> People go to Sinn Féin advice centers; there is a network of these centers. It is up to a two year process. There is a tariff system. With respect to the length of exclusion, it can be three months, six months, or one year. You can be ordered out of the country or it can be both kneecaps or just one.[325]

John, a Catholic, told Human Rights Watch/Helsinki that he was expelled from Northern Ireland in 1989 *after* a punishment attack:

> Me and my brother were taken out of a bar by three guys wearing masks. They said they were from the IRA. They took us to a house across the street and brought me into the back. There were five people in the house and they tied me up and tied my brother up. They beat me with a bat and with cudgels with nails in them.
>
> I went to hospital and my parents were already there. Three days later, the IRA came and told my parents, "If your four sons are not out in forty-eight hours. . ." They said we know what it's

---

[324]Human Rights Watch/Helsinki, *Children in Northern Ireland*, p. 50.

[325]Human Rights Watch/Helsinki interview, Belfast, November 14, 1996.

for. We left and went to Manchester, England. I was twenty-three and had to stay out. My parents went to Connolly House on the Falls Road.[326] I had to stay out for one year, eight months. I had two younger brothers and one older. They had to be out for one and a half years. I came back three months later but had to move out of Belfast. It happens all over but you can move to other areas.[327]

Expulsion orders are often issued without warning and in the absence of the alleged perpetrator. These ultimatums are crude trials *in absentia* during which members of paramilitary organizations determine an alleged perpetrator's guilt and hand down a sentence of exile:

•   In July 1996, it was reported that four masked men—two carrying handguns—entered a house in Armagh and told a man inside that another man, who they called by name, had forty-eight hours to leave the country.[328]

•   Four masked men reportedly entered the home of a Ballymagroarty man in August 1996 wielding guns and cudgels and told the man's family that he had forty-eight hours to leave London/Derry.[329]

•   Seven men between the ages of seventeen and thirty were expelled by the IRA in September 1996 after an evening of destruction in a west Belfast housing estate which included the burning of eight cars and a fast food business was attributed to them.[330]

---

[326]A Sinn Féin advice center.

[327]Human Rights Watch/Helsinki interview, Belfast, November 21, 1996.

[328]"North Man Told to Quit Country," *Irish Times*, July 26, 1996.

[329]"RUC Investigates Ultimatum Claim," *Irish Times*, August 29, 1996.

[330]Brendan Anderson and Phelim McAleer, "Expulsions Ordered after 'Orgy of Violence,'" *Irish News*, September 27, 1996. This case of mass expulsion occurred after a prolonged period of tension in the Poleglass area during which young men drank and engaged in joyriding on a weekly basis throughout the area. Local residents were said to be

In loyalist areas, expulsions are frequently used as disciplinary measures within a paramilitary organization or they can be used to settle scores between feuding paramilitary groups. The most public of loyalist expulsion orders was issued in September 1996 when two well-known loyalist paramilitaries were ordered to leave Northern Ireland in the name of the Combined Loyalist Military Command (CLMC), the loyalist paramilitary umbrella organization responsible for calling the loyalist cease-fire in October 1994.

The two paramilitaries, Billy Wright of the Mid-Ulster UVF and Alex Kerr, then in prison on remand, were ordered in the name of the CLMC to "quit Ulster or die."[331] The CLMC demanded that Wright leave Northern Ireland within seventy-two hours and Kerr leave immediately upon release from prison. Both men were said to have defied CLMC orders.

Requirements of International Law

International humanitarian law applies to the conduct of paramilitary groups in Northern Ireland. A core principle of international humanitarian law is the protection of civilians in armed conflict, as well as others taking no part in hostilities including combatants who have been captured or are otherwise hors de combat. The four Geneva Conventions of 1949 regulate the conduct of parties to international armed conflict. Article 3, common to all four conventions, sets out minimum standards for the treatment of civilians and others taking no active part in the hostilities during armed conflicts "not of an international character."[332]

---

terrified of the group. A week after the violence which led to the expulsions, an RUC spokesman told reporters that the police force had "no knowledge of the damage or the expulsions." Ibid.

[331]Vivek Chaudhary, "Senior Loyalists 'On Hit List,'" *The Guardian*, September 6, 1996. Billy Wright is currently serving a prison sentence for threatening to kill a woman.

[332]Common Article 3 states:
In the case of armed conflict not of an international character occurring in the territory of one of the high contracting parties, each party to the conflict shall be bound to apply, as a minimum, the following provisions:
(1) Persons taking no active part in the hostilities, including members of armed forces who have laid down their arms and those placed *hors de combat* by sickness, wounds, detention, or any other cause, shall in all circumstances be treated humanely, without any adverse distinction founded on race, colour, religion or faith, sex birth or wealth, or any

Common Article 3 requires that civilians and other protected persons in internal armed conflicts be treated humanely, with specific prohibitions on murder, torture, or cruel, humiliating or degrading treatment.[333] It also forbids the passing of sentences and carrying out of executions without previous judgment pronounced by a regularly constituted court without due process of law. Common Article 3 is binding on all parties to a conflict, including both government and opposition forces. The U.K. is a signatory to the Geneva Conventions and thus is bound by their provisions; authoritative interpretations of Common Article 3, in turn, have found that insurgent forces are also bound by these provisions.[334]

---

similar criteria.

To this end, the following acts are and shall remain prohibited at any time and in any place whatsoever with respect to the above-mentioned persons:

> (a) violence to life and person, in particular murder of all kinds, mutilation, cruel treatment, and torture;
>
> (b) taking of hostages;
>
> © outrages upon personal dignity, in particular humiliating and degrading treatment;
>
> (d) the passing of sentences and the carrying out of executions without previous judgement pronounced by a regularly constituted court, affording all the judicial guarantees which are recognizable as indispensable by civilized peoples.

(2) The wounded and sick shall be collected and cared for.

[333] Amnesty International has characterized punishment assaults and shootings as torture or ill-treatment. It has also condemned killings by paramilitary organizations of its own members. In February 1994, AI called on the leadership of all paramilitary organizations in Northern Ireland "to ensure that their members: don't torture, don't kill prisoners, don't kill civilians, [and] don't take hostages." See Amnesty International, *Political Killings in Northern Ireland*, February 1994, pp. 69-70.

[334] Jean S. Pictet, ed., *Commentary on III Geneva Convention Relative to the Treatment of Prisoners of War* (Geneva: International Committee of the Red Cross, 1960), pp. 37-38:

> The words "each Party" mark a step forward in international law. Until recently it would have been considered impossible in law for an international Convention to bind a non-signatory Party—a Party, moreover, which was not yet in existence and which need not even represent a legal entity capable of undertaking international obligations. It had not been thought possible to conclude an agreement without

There has been some debate about whether or not the conflict in Northern Ireland meets the requirements of an "internal armed conflict."[335] Human Rights Watch/Helsinki believes that the situation in Northern Ireland is governed by the Geneva Convention's minimum standards for internal armed conflicts. Support for this position can be found in the International Committee of the Red Cross's well-respected commentary[336] which indicates that Common Article 3 should be applied as broadly as possible in situations of armed conflict. Some delegates to the diplomatic conference responsible for drafting the Geneva Conventions suggested a set of criteria to distinguish "a genuine armed conflict" from other types of

---

reciprocal undertakings and such undertakings would imply that the contracting parties were already in existence. As we have seen, however, the present Convention no longer includes a reciprocity clause. This great step forward cleared the way for the provisions of Article 3...

...what justification is there for the obligation on the adverse Party in revolt against the established authority? Doubts have been expressed on this subject. How could insurgents be legally bound by a Convention which they had not themselves signed? But if the responsible authority at their head exercises effective sovereignty, it is bound by the very fact that it claims to represent the country, or part of the country.

If an insurgent party applies Article 3, so much the better for the victims of the conflict. No one will complain. If it does not apply it, it will prove that those who regard its actions as mere acts of anarchy or brigandage are right. As for the *de jure* government, the effect on it of applying Article 3 cannot be in any way prejudicial; for no government can possibly claim that it is *entitled* to make use of torture and other inhumane acts prohibited by the Convention, as a means of combatting its enemies.

[335]See Boyle and Campbell, *Human Rights Work in Situations of Armed Conflict and Political Violence: Northern Ireland*, p. 26-32.

[336]Jean S. Pictet, ed., *Commentary on IV Geneva Convention Relative to the Protection of Civilian Persons in Time of War* (Geneva: International Committee of the Red Cross, 1958).

conflicts.[337] The conference, however, abandoned the idea of a clear definition in favor of a broad application of Common Article 3:

> Does this mean that Article 3 is not applicable in cases where armed strife breaks out in a country, but does not fulfil any of the above conditions (which are not obligatory and are only mentioned as an indication)? We do not subscribe to this view. We think, on the contrary, that the scope of the application of the Article must be as wide as possible. There can be no drawbacks in this, since the Article in its reduced form, contrary to what may be thought, does not in any way limit the right of a State to put down rebellion, nor does it increase in the slightest the authority of the rebel party. It merely demands respect for certain rules, which were already recognized as essential in all civilized countries, and embodied in the municipal law of the States in question, long before the Convention was signed. What Government would dare to claim before the world, in a case of civil disturbances which could justly be described as mere acts of banditry, that Article 3 not being applicable, it was entitled to leave the wounded uncared for, to torture and mutilate prisoners and take hostages? However useful, therefore, the various conditions stated above may be, they are not indispensable, since no Government can object to observing, in its dealings with internal enemies, whatever the nature of the conflict between it and them, a few essential rules which it in fact observes daily, under its own laws, even when dealing with common criminals.[338]

---

[337]Ibid., pp. 35-36. The need to establish criteria arose from the fear of some delegates that "armed conflict" might be interpreted as "any form of anarchy, rebellion, or even plain banditry." Although withdrawn in the end, the suggested criteria included that the party in revolt possess an organized military force, have control over a specified territory, have an organization purporting to have the characteristics of a state, and agree to be bound by the provisions of the convention. The legal government would have been required *inter alia* to recognize the insurgents.

[338]Ibid., p. 36

Paramilitary punishment assaults and shootings thus violate the right to life, freedom from humiliating and degrading treatment, the right to due process and the guarantee of a fair trial as codified in Common Article 3.[339]

---

[339]The punishments phenomenon is also prohibited by customary international humanitarian law. In an important 1986 decision, the International Court of Justice held that the rules defined in Common Article 3:

> also constitute a minimum yardstick, in addition to the more elaborate rules which are also to apply to international conflicts; and that they are rules which . . . reflect what the Court in 1949 called "elementary considerations of humanity."

International Court of Justice, *Reports of Judgments, Advisory Opinions and Orders*. Nicaragua v. United States of America. Merits, Judgment of 27 June 1986, p. 114, para. 218. Cited in *International Review of the Red Cross* (Geneva: International Committee of the Red Cross, September-October 1990), p. 386. According to this holding, the rules in Common Article 3 are customary international law and, as such, constitute basic, minimum standards applicable in all situations of armed conflict and binding on all parties to a conflict.

6. ALLEGATIONS OF COLLUSION BETWEEN MEMBERS OF THE SECURITY FORCES AND LOYALIST PARAMILITARY ORGANIZATIONS

Introduction

Allegations of collusion between members of the security forces in Northern Ireland and loyalist paramilitary groups continue to be leveled at the RUC and the British military. Collusion is generally defined as a secret agreement or cooperation for an illegal or deceitful purpose.[340] In Northern Ireland, members of the security forces are alleged to engage in collusion by conspiring directly with loyalist paramilitaries to carry out acts of violence or by facilitating the commission of violent activities. The failure to prevent or deter violent acts for which there is reliable advance intelligence or to investigate rigorously such acts and punish those responsible can also constitute collusion. Those who allege collusion charge that members of the security forces routinely engage in a variety of illegal activities to assist loyalist paramilitary groups to target suspected republican "terrorists" or alleged "terrorist" sympathizers for harassment and assassination.[341] In addition to allegations of direct involvement in the planning and execution of assassinations, actions by security forces that can constitute collusion include:[342]

---

[340] *Webster's New Collegiate Dictionary* (Springfield, Massachusetts: G. & C. Merriam Company, 1981), p. 219.

[341] For example, Father Raymond Murray told Helsinki Watch in 1991 that he believes killings by security forces in Northern Ireland fall into three categories: deliberate, professional killings by the SAS (British Army Special Air Services Regiment, an elite unit charged with intelligence gathering and surveillance), killings by "trigger happy bully boys" who harass people and create violent situations that can result in shootings, and cases of collusion, in which security forces pass information to paramilitaries, who then shoot and kill suspected terrorists. See Helsinki Watch, *Human Rights in Northern Ireland*, p. 49. See also Raymond Murray, *The SAS in Ireland* (Mercier Press, Dublin, 1990). The government of the United Kingdom has denied a "shoot to kill" policy in Northern Ireland. However, the government has admitted collusion between some members of the security forces and loyalist paramilitary groups. (See section below titled "Stevens Inquiry.")

[342] Some human rights groups allege that collusion is systemic implicating all the arms of the state responsible for the administration of justice in Northern Ireland. It is generally observed that when security forces are found directly or indirectly to have assisted loyalist paramilitaries, the director of public prosecutions and the secretary of state for Northern Ireland fail to hold those responsible for collusion accountable, declining to

139

- Passing on security information such as photo montages, house floor plans, car registration numbers, and other security identification information to loyalist paramilitaries who use the information to target suspected republican "terrorists" (or alleged "terrorist" sympathizers) for harassment or assassination.

- Facilitating the commission of loyalist paramilitary killings by diverting law enforcement resources away from crime scenes immediately prior to and after paramilitary shootings, denying essential medical personnel access to shooting victims, and lifting roadblocks.

- Failing to provide adequate protection to persons warned by the security forces that they are under threat because their security files or other identification information accidentally went missing or were stolen and are in the hands of loyalist paramilitaries.

- Failing to investigate rigorously loyalist paramilitary killings by overlooking critical and easily accessible forensic evidence, failing to interview eyewitnesses, and generally avoiding any concerted effort to apprehend a suspect or suspects.

- Providing firearms and other weapons to loyalist paramilitaries.

Human Rights Watch/Helsinki is particularly concerned with allegations of collusion against the police force in Northern Ireland. The Royal Ulster Constabulary is invested with primary responsibility for identifying, gathering and securing information on suspected paramilitaries and investigating acts of

---

prosecute or discipline perpetrators, issuing "public interest immunity certificates" (which exempt security force personnel from testifying) to suppress evidence of collusion on grounds of "national security" in judicial proceedings and at inquests, and refusing to make public the findings of internal inquiries into allegations of collusion within the security apparatus. See British Irish Rights Watch, *Alleged Collusion and the RUC* (London: BIRW, November 1996), pp. 1-2.

paramilitary violence.[343] Thus, the police force is particularly susceptible to charges of collusion, especially when legitimately collected official information finds its way into the hands of loyalist paramilitaries. RUC management told Human Rights Watch/Helsinki that there have been "remarkably few" cases of police officers passing information on to loyalist paramilitaries but in those cases which *have* been spotted over the last twenty-five years, those individuals have been "dealt with."[344] In fact, there has never been an acknowledged criminal or disciplinary charge leveled against an RUC officer for collusion;[345] thus it remains unclear when, how and under what circumstances officers involved in collusion have been "dealt with."

The RUC categorically denies allegations that collusion is systemic, claiming that collusion, if it does occur, is carried out by particular individuals on the ground and is in no way institutionalized.[346] By espousing the "bad apple" theory—which suggests that individual officers may be deviant[347] but the RUC as an institution maintains its integrity and impartiality—the RUC assumes the

---

[343]The British army and the locally recruited Ulster Defense Regiment (UDR) provide support for the RUC under the U.K. government's policy of "police primacy" for the management of the security regime. The principle of police primacy was established in 1976 and gave the RUC "ultimate control of security forces activity in Northern Ireland." See Urban, *Big Boys' Rules*, p.12.

[344]Human Rights Watch/Helsinki interview with RUC Chief Constable Ronnie Flanagan, Belfast, November 11, 1996.

[345]Letter from Ronald Flanagan, RUC chief constable, to Human Rights Watch/Helsinki, March 7, 1997.

[346]Human Rights Watch/Helsinki interview, Belfast, November 11, 1996.

[347]See Paddy Hillyard, "The Politics of Policing and Policing Itself: The Stalker Affair," Paper presented at an international conference on "Policing the Peace," University College Galway, August 23-25, 1995, p. 11. Hillyard suggests three broad theories to explain illegal police conduct in miscarriage of justice cases and in cases where the RUC has been alleged to espouse a "shoot to kill" policy. The "bad apple" theory focuses on the individual officer as deviant. The "bad barrel theory" critiques police culture and organization and suggests that illegal police conduct naturally occurs within law enforcement agencies. The "rotten orchard theory" suggests that deviant police conduct does not arise from within the force, but originates "in structures of dominance" within the larger society. Thus, the integrity of the chief constable and the police force are prioritized over the rule of law or the search for justice. Ibid.

untenable position of conceding that it cannot exercise sufficient control over all its officers and security procedures while, at the same time, it disclaims any responsibility for the loyalist killings of members of the minority Catholic community, be they nationalist, republican, or indifferent, due to that lack of control.

Collusion, by definition, is difficult to prove. Human Rights Watch/Helsinki makes no conclusions regarding the evidence of collusion against the RUC in any of the cases highlighted in this report. However, the factors suggesting the possibility of collusion associated with each case compel us to call for a variety of immediate official responses to determine whether or not collusion actually occurred. In some cases an independent inquiry with full investigative powers, including the power to subpoena witnesses and documents, is recommended. In other cases, we call on the RUC to take specific steps to ensure that factors suggesting collusion are adequately addressed. General recommendations by which the RUC can effectively address allegations of collusion include: a thorough reassessment of security procedures and the handling of identification information for security breaches; vetting recruits, officers, and reservists of the police force for associations with loyalist paramilitary groups; greater transparency in the investigation of loyalist paramilitary killings; commitment to rigorous investigations of paramilitary killings in conformity with international standards; and a review of inquest procedures in Northern Ireland which appear designed to deny families access to information.

Human Rights Watch/Helsinki met with RUC management, the families of victims of loyalist paramilitary assassinations, politicians, government officials, human rights activists, the coroner for Greater Belfast, defense lawyers, and others to discuss allegations of collusion. We review outstanding cases where collusion has been alleged and highlight recent cases which suggest that the debate over collusion is ongoing as questions continue to arise regarding the nature, depth and consequences of possible state complicity in loyalist paramilitary activities.

Background

In 1989, an illegal loyalist paramilitary group, the Ulster Freedom Fighters (UFF), claimed responsibility for two murders. Both killings—one of a suspected IRA member and the other of a prominent Catholic defense lawyer—involved factors that strongly suggested security force participation in the killings and brought the issue of collusion into the public domain beyond the confines of Northern Ireland. A subsequent government review—the Stevens Inquiry— focused on allegations of collusion between members of the security forces and loyalist paramilitaries and concluded that collusion between the two groups had occurred. Since then, human rights groups and others have documented numerous cases which suggest security force involvement and have called on the government of the United Kingdom to address such allegations effectively, apparently to no avail.[348]

The Stevens Inquiry

In August 1989, the UFF claimed responsibility for the murder of a Catholic man, Loughlin Maginn, and justified the killing by claiming that Maginn was an IRA member.[349] The paramilitary group publicly stated that official documents had been passed to them indicating that Maginn was a suspected IRA member. It was confirmed within weeks that security documents were missing from two security bases. Over the next few months, the press reported that official security information on members of the nationalist community, including hundreds of photographs, files, personal information, house layouts, and car registration numbers had been leaked to loyalist paramilitaries. RUC Chief Constable Hugh Annesley appointed John Stevens, a senior British police officer, to conduct an independent investigation of allegations of security leaks which became known as the Stevens Inquiry.

The full report from the Stevens Inquiry was never made public. A summary of the report was released in May 1990 and concluded that collusion had, in fact, occurred:

> It is clear that official information, originally produced by the
> Royal Ulster Constabulary, the Army and the Prison Service, has

---

[348]See Lawyers Committee for Human Rights, *At the Crossroads: Human Rights and the Northern Ireland Peace Process*, 1996 and *Human Rights and Legal Defense in Northern* Ireland, 1933; British Irish Rights Watch, *Alleged Collusion and the RUC*, November 1996; Relatives for Justice, *Collusion 1990-1994: Loyalist Paramilitary Murders in North of Ireland* (London/Derry: RFJ, 1995) and *Shoot-to-Kill and Collusion* (London/Derry: RFJ, July 1993); Amnesty International, *Political Killings in Northern Ireland* (London: AI, February 1994); Committee on the Administration of Justice, *Adding Insult to Injury? Allegations of Harassment and the Use of Lethal Force by the Security Forces in Northern Ireland* (Belfast: CAJ, December 1993). Members of various United Nations bodies, including Dr. Claire Palley, the independent expert nominated by the government of the United Kingdom to the U.N. Sub-Commission on the Prevention of Discrimination and the Protection of Minorities, have also expressed concern about the U.K.'s inadequate response to allegations of collusion.

[349]Helsinki Watch, *Human Rights in Northern Ireland*, p. 61.

passed, illicitly, into the hands of the loyalist paramilitary groups. Documents and information from documents have been traced to the possession of these paramilitaries. They have been used by them to enhance their own intelligence systems and as an aid to the targeting of persons suspected of being Republican terrorists.[350]

Stevens also concluded:

It is clear from the evidence and detailed analysis of the Security Force documents recovered during the Enquiry, that the passing of information to paramilitaries by members of the Security Forces is restricted to a small number of individuals and is neither widespread nor institutionalised.[351]

Two Ulster Defense Regiment (UDR) soldiers were charged with the murder of Loughlin Maginn and given life sentences in March 1992 for passing security information to loyalist paramilitaries who used it to target Maginn.[352] The Stevens Inquiry resulted in ninety-four arrests with fifty-nine people charged or reported to the director for public prosecutions. There were forty-six prosecutions and 183 convictions for separate offences,[353] including the unauthorized communication of security information to loyalist paramilitaries, the unlawful possession of official documents, and the collection and recording of classified information.[354] Notably, most of those convicted were members of paramilitary groups, the recipients of security information. The rest were part-time members of the UDR, many of whom were believed to be associated with loyalist paramilitary organizations. Despite the fact that many of the documents leaked to

---

[350]*Summary of the Report of the Deputy Chief Constable of Cambridgeshire John Stevens, into Allegations of Collusion between Members of the Security Forces and Loyalist Paramilitaries*, May 17, 1990, para. 27, p. 12. (Stevens Inquiry)

[351]Ibid., para. 11, pp. 5-6.

[352]Amnesty International, *Political Killings in Northern Ireland*, p. 23.

[353]British Irish Rights Watch, *Alleged Collusion and the RUC*, p. 6.

[354]Amnesty International, *Political Killings in Northern Ireland*, p. 24.

paramilitaries were from police files, not a single police officer was charged. Stevens justified the absence of charges against the RUC by noting that exchanges of security information between various arms of the security regime was inevitable but the "lack of any mechanism for accounting for the movement of such material [has] contributed to the difficulties in tracing those responsible for passing on information illegally."[355] He stated:

> It could not, for example, be assumed that a document found in the possession of a terrorist organisation which was headed 'Royal Ulster Constabulary,' 'Army' or 'Prison Service' was leaked directly from that particular element of the Security Forces.[356]

Of the eighty-three recommendations contained in the Stevens Inquiry report, thirty-one of them were directed at the RUC. Most of the recommendations addressed the production and tracking of photo montages and the strict control of crime scene evidence, including finger prints and exhibits.[357] The narrow scope of the Stevens Inquiry, focused as it was on the handling of security information, failed to address the wider allegations of security force participation in loyalist paramilitary killings. As Amnesty International noted:

> It [the Stevens Inquiry] did not look at evidence that collusion between members of the security forces and Loyalist armed groups had been going on for many years or at the overall pattern as it related to both targeted and random killings of Catholics. It did not examine the authorities' record during this time in bringing criminal proceedings against security personnel in this regard, or the official response to evidence of partiality and discriminatory treatment, for example, soldiers shouting verbal abuse at Catholics or writing sectarian graffiti on walls.[358]

---

[355]Stevens Inquiry, para. 7, p. 4.

[356]Ibid.

[357]Ibid., pp. 23-29.

[358]Amnesty International, *Political Killings in Northern Ireland*, p. 25.

The Stevens Inquiry concluded that, in the context of the Northern Ireland conflict, leakages of information from the security forces may never be eliminated.[359]

The Murder of Patrick Finucane

Patrick Finucane was a thirty-nine year old Catholic criminal defense lawyer who gained prominence representing persons detained under Northern Ireland's emergency legislation.[360] Along with his law partner, Peter Madden, Finucane regularly, and often successfully, challenged human rights abuses related to the emergency laws.[361] This work made him the target of abuse from a number of quarters, including within the RUC. In addition to credible evidence that RUC detectives frequently targeted Finucane for verbal abuse, escalating to death threats in the months before his murder,[362] a government minister publicly singled out solicitors in Northern Ireland who were "unduly sympathetic to the cause of the IRA" in parliament three weeks before Patrick Finucane was killed. As we noted in our 1991 report *Human Rights in Northern Ireland*, the minister, Douglas Hogg, was severely criticized by many who felt that his words could stimulate violence against lawyers who were fulfilling their responsibilities in representing accused persons in the courts.[363]

On February 12, 1989, Patrick Finucane was killed by two masked gunmen who entered his home and shot him repeatedly in front of his wife and three children. He was shot a total of fourteen times. His wife, Geraldine Finucane, was injured when a bullet probably ricocheted and hit her in the ankle. The UFF claimed responsibility for the murder but no one has ever been charged for the act.

In its 1993 report, *Human Rights and Legal Defense in Northern Ireland*, the Lawyers Committee for Human Rights presented evidence highly suggestive

---

[359]Stevens Inquiry, para. 10, p. 5.

[360]Helsinki Watch, *Human Rights in Northern Ireland*, pp. 100-104.

[361]For a sample of Patrick Finucane's legal successes, see Lawyers Committee for Human Rights, *Human Rights and Legal Defense in Northern Ireland*, pp. 43-45.

[362]Helsinki Watch, *Human Rights in Northern Ireland*, 1991, p. 101. See also Amnesty International, *United Kingdom Human Rights Concerns* (London: AI, June 1991).

[363]Helsinki Watch, *Human Rights in Northern Ireland*, p. 101

of official collusion in the murder of Patrick Finucane. The Lawyers Committee alleged that both the British army and the RUC may have been complicit in the murder. In 1987, British military intelligence recruited a man named Brian Nelson as an agent. Nelson served as chief intelligence officer for then legal Ulster Defense Association (UDA) and was responsible for providing army intelligence with details about loyalist paramilitary activities, including planned assassinations, which the army would then pass on to the RUC. In fact, a number of loyalist murders that Nelson helped plan actually took place. According to the Lawyers Committee, "It remains unclear to this day whether this occurred because Nelson 'got out of hand,' because the Army hoarded its information out of a sense of rivalry with the RUC, or because of some other reason." [364]

In January 1990, Nelson was arrested and eventually convicted of conspiracy to murder and sentenced to ten years in prison.[365] A BBC *Panorama* documentary, broadcast on June 8, 1992, subsequently revealed that Nelson had written in his prison journal that he had informed "his handlers" that Patrick Finucane was being targeted by loyalist paramilitaries as early as December 1988.[366] The journal also revealed that Nelson had passed a photograph of Patrick Finucane on to a paramilitary assassin a few days before the murder.[367] Although the RUC denied that any information the army received from Brian Nelson about the impending murder of Patrick Finucane was passed on to the police, a witness at Nelson's trial contradicted this denial. Colonel "J", a senior ranking military intelligence officer, testified at trial that Nelson provided him with UDA materials on a weekly basis. These materials included security documents, photo montages, and reports "from all sectors of the security forces" which had been leaked to the

---

[364]Lawyers Committee for Human Rights, *Human Rights and Legal Defense in Northern Ireland*, p. 53.

[365]Nelson's prosecution and conviction were an outcome of the Stevens Inquiry. Many human rights activists were dismayed by the light sentence Nelson received. See British Irish Rights Watch, *Alleged Collusion and the RUC*, pp.7-8.

[366]Lawyers Committee for Human Rights, *Human Rights and Legal Defense in Northern Ireland*, p. 53.

[367]Ibid.

UDA. Colonel "J" also testified that the information provided to military intelligence by Brian Nelson was passed on to the RUC.[368]

In a 1996 report that includes an update on developments in the Finucane murder, the Lawyers Committee expressed dismay that no prosecutions had arisen from the revelations in the Nelson prison journal or the *Panorama* program.[369] This disappointment was acute, especially in light of the request by then RUC Chief Constable Hugh Annesley that John Stevens, the senior police officer who conducted the first Stevens Inquiry, investigate the allegations made in the *Panorama* program. Stevens issued his final report to the director of public prosecutions in January 1995. It was on February 17, 1995, that the DPP issued a direction of "no prosecution" to the chief constable.[370] The Lawyers Committee noted:

> Information brought to light by the BBC's *Panorama* program revealed that Nelson not only helped in Finucane's murder, but that he had made his Army handlers aware of the plan. This information provided the strongest evidence of a possible link between loyalist paramilitaries who took credit for the killing and elements within the security forces. In this light, the DPP's decision not to bring further prosecutions in connection with Nelson's activities closes the Finucane case for all realistic intents and purposes.[371]

The report from the second Stevens Inquiry was not made public nor was a summary available. The Lawyers Committee interviewed John Stevens in London in August 1995 to discuss the findings of the Nelson investigation and the DPP's decision not to prosecute. Stevens stated that "any wrongdoing he unearthed would have been turned over to the RUC for evaluation and then to the DPP for

---

[368]Amnesty International, *Political Killings in Northern Ireland*, p. 27.

[369]Lawyers Committee for Human Rights, *At the Crossroads: Human Rights and the Northern Ireland Peace Process*, p. 108.

[370]British Irish Rights Watch, *Alleged Collusion and the RUC*, p. 8.

[371]Lawyers Committee for Human Rights, *At the Crossroads: Human Rights and the Northern Ireland Peace Process*, p. 108.

prosecution."[372] Stevens declined to discuss whether or not he recommended prosecutions in his report claiming he was prohibited from commenting by the Official Secrets Act.[373] Most notably, Stevens told the Lawyers Committee that he knew "absolutely" who killed Patrick Finucane, "but was not at liberty to disclose their identity publicly."[374]

At a meeting in November 1996, Human Rights Watch/Helsinki questioned Alasdair Fraser, the director of public prosecutions, about Nelson's allegations and the DPP's decision not to prosecute. The DPP told us that he "can't answer completely" any questions about the Nelson affair.[375] However, Fraser stated that the second Stevens Inquiry had concluded that there was "insufficient evidence to warrant prosecution of any person."[376] Moreover, Daniel Magill, deputy director for the DPP, told Human Rights Watch/Helsinki that "If there had been evidence sufficient to prosecute Brian Nelson for the murder of Pat Finucane, he'd have been prosecuted."[377]

It remains unclear why the DPP would tell Human Rights Watch/Helsinki that the report from the second Stevens Inquiry recommended no prosecutions but Stevens himself felt compelled to invoke the Official Secrets Act in order to avoid answering the question regarding prosecutions put to him by the Lawyers Committee in 1995. It also remains unclear why Brian Nelson's own admission of involvement in Patrick Finucane's murder was considered "insufficient" to bring a prosecution against him.

Geraldine Finucane has brought a civil action against the United Kingdom Ministry of Defense and Brian Nelson for wrongful death. Mrs. Finucane alleges that Nelson and his British army intelligence "handlers" knew that Patrick Finucane had been targeted by loyalist paramilitaries and thus were negligent in failing to take preventive action to stop his murder. According to Peter Madden, Mrs. Finucane's lawyer, the civil case has been stalled by the government's reluctance

---

[372]Ibid., p. 110.

[373]Ibid.

[374]Ibid.

[375]Human Rights Watch/Helsinki interview, Belfast, November 12, 1996.

[376]Ibid.

[377]Ibid.

to grant the discovery of documents relevant to the case.[378] Some documents have been produced but have been edited heavily.

Mrs. Finucane has also lodged an application with the European Commission for Human Rights arguing that the United Kingdom failed to guarantee Patrick Finucane the "right to life" under article 2 of the European Convention for Human Rights. According to Peter Madden, the British government's defense—that Nelson got "out of control" and began to operate independently—does not explain the government's failure to take preventive measures to protect Patrick Finucane especially as it had reliable intelligence that a credible threat to life existed.[379]

Human Rights Watch/Helsinki joins Amnesty International, the Lawyers Committee, and Dr. Claire Palley, the independent expert nominated by the U.K. government to the U.N. Sub-Commission on the Prevention of Discrimination and the Protection of Minorities, in calling for an independent, public inquiry—with powers to administer oaths and to subpoena witnesses and documents—into the killing of Patrick Finucane. We strongly condemn the failure of state authorities to pursue criminal prosecutions for the murder and urge the government of the United Kingdom to cease efforts to suppress information related to the case.

Recent Developments

From 1990 onward, Human Rights Watch/Helsinki and other human rights groups have received reliable reports of loyalist paramilitary killings marked by factors suggesting official collusion in the murders. As well, a number of killings which took place in the late 1980s are only now being scheduled for inquests giving families new impetus to review cases and bring their concerns to a coroner and jury charged with impartiality. Unfortunately, the narrow remit of the inquest system in Northern Ireland, bolstered by judicial support for limitations on the scope of the inquiry undertaken at inquests, has made it extremely difficult to enter evidence of collusion into inquest proceedings.

The Murder of Patrick Shanaghan

Patrick Shanaghan was driving his van to his job at the Department of Environment (DOE) in Castlederg, County Tyrone, on August 12, 1991, at 8:20 a.m. when a lone masked gunman riddled the van with a hail of bullets from a semi-automatic weapon. According to police logs, Patrick Shanaghan was

---

[378]Human Rights Watch/Helsinki interview, Belfast, November 8, 1996.

[379]Ibid.

pronounced officially dead by a doctor at approximately 9:50 a.m. The UFF claimed responsibility for the murder. However, the sequence of events from the time of the shooting until the collapse of the inquest nearly five years later— coupled with a ten-year history of constant harassment of Patrick Shanaghan by UDR and RUC officers—indicate that allegations of security force participation in the murder have not been addressed adequately by the RUC or the government of the United Kingdom. Patrick Shanaghan's murder involved a number of signature characteristics associated with murders by collusion and provides a case study of how the criminal justice system in Northern Ireland is perceived to shield collaboration between illegal loyalist paramilitary groups and those responsible for the administration of justice.

RUC suspicions of IRA membership resulted in a long campaign of harassment directed at Patrick Shanaghan, his family and his friends. Patrick Shanaghan was a thirty-three-year-old Catholic and active member of Sinn Féin, a legally recognized political party, when he was killed. Despite RUC allegations that he was an IRA member, there was no evidence that Patrick Shanaghan had any connection with the IRA. Most notably, his funeral was absent the traditional IRA honor guard or any sign of IRA membership.

RUC records indicate that Patrick Shanaghan was arrested ten times between April 1985 and May 1991. Six of the ten arrests resulted in detentions for four or more days.[380] Patrick Shanaghan was never charged with any crime. He gave several written statements to his solicitors alleging physical assaults by RUC detectives while in detention, including being punched in the back, punched under the chin with a clenched fist, stabbed in the throat with extended fingers (martial arts style), slapped in the face,[381] having his arms wrenched back and forth repeatedly,[382] forced to stand in a crouched position for hours, having his head struck against a wall, and being hit and kicked in the testicles.[383] On several occasions, according to his sworn statements, RUC detectives conducting

---

[380]Letter from RUC to Porter & McCanny, Patrick Shanaghan's solicitors, dated August 23, 1991.

[381]Signed statement from Patrick Shanaghan to Porter & McCanny, August 3, 1988.

[382]Signed statement from Patrick Shanaghan to Porter & McCanny, May 16, 1990.

[383]Signed statement from Patrick Shanaghan to Porter & McCanny, March 3, 1988.

interrogations of Patrick Shanaghan verbally abused him and threatened him with death, for example, by telling him that "Loyalists in Castlederg know you now and they will get you."[384]

The Shanaghan family home, which Patrick shared with his mother, Mary, was searched sixteen times between 1985 and 1991. Nothing was ever found in the home. Mary Shanaghan told Human Rights Watch/Helsinki that sometimes the RUC would not even enter certain rooms indicating that the search was not a concerted effort to locate and seize illegal material but was used solely to harass the Shanaghan family.[385] Patrick Shanaghan was stopped and questioned by RUC and UDR officers on a daily basis. He was often told to remove his jacket, especially in cold weather.[386] A co-worker at the DOE stated that he was the only person who would work with Patrick because all the others feared that they would be shot.[387]

On February 17, 1989, an attempt was made on Patrick Shanaghan's life. As he was leaving his house at approximately 8:00 p.m. that evening, eight shots were fired at him.[388] He managed to escape into nearby fields while being shot at. Returning to his house after a time, he noticed a car traveling slowly away from the house. Patrick Shanaghan phoned the RUC, which arrived forty-five minutes later. No charges have been brought against a suspect for the murder attempt. When Patrick Shanaghan was arrested in February 1990, he publicly stated that

---

[384]Signed statement from Patrick Shanaghan to Porter & McCanny, dated August 3, 1988. See also, "Three Accuse Police After Interrogation," *The Ulster Herald*, February 24, 1990.

[385]Human Rights Watch/Helsinki interview, Limavady, November 21, 1996.

[386]Ibid.

[387]Written statement from Gerry Keenan to the Inquiry into the Killing of Patrick Shanaghan, September 17-19, 1996. This three day public inquiry was sponsored by the Castlederg Aghyaran Justice Group and included testimony from the official inquest, evidence suppressed at the inquest, and testimony from expert witnesses on topics such as collusion in Northern Ireland and the inquest system. The Hon. Andrew Somers, a retired U.S. judge, presided over the proceedings. See Caitriona Ruane, "Public Inquiry into the Death of Patrick Shanaghan," *Just News: Bulletin of the Committee on the Administration of Justice*, vol. 11, no. 10, October 1996, pp. 6-7.

[388]Handwritten and signed statement from Patrick Shanaghan to Porter & McCanny, re: events of February 17, 1989, undated.

RUC officers repeatedly mentioned this murder attempt during interrogation and one detective claimed, "we won't miss next time."[389]

The RUC warned Patrick Shanaghan twice that he was under threat from loyalist paramilitary groups. In December 1990, RUC detectives informed him that security force documentation containing his personal information, including a photo montage, had fallen out the back of an army vehicle and into the hands of loyalist paramilitaries. A letter dated January 11, 1991, was sent to the RUC by Patrick Shanaghan's solicitors who requested, "as a matter of urgency" in order to assess the risk to Patrick Shanaghan and his family, information relating to the documentation including the type of information lost, dates the information was first recorded, the exact date and under what circumstances it went missing, copies of photographs and addresses included in the files, and information in relation to the social movement and employment of persons involved in handling the files.[390] On July 29, 1994, nearly three years after Patrick Shanaghan's murder, the RUC responded to this letter by stating, "The police investigation is concluded. The document was accidentally lost by the Army."[391] The RUC warned Patrick Shanaghan again in April 1991, four months before he was killed, that he was under paramilitary threat. According to Martin Bogues, Patrick Shanaghan's brother-in-law, the RUC officer who informed Patrick of the threat refused to offer the grounds upon which the warning was based.[392]

British Irish Rights Watch maintains that RUC warnings about personal safety in circumstances where official security information has gone missing, often "look more like threats than any attempt to protect the victim."[393] RUC Chief

---

[389]"Three Accuse Police after Interrogation," *The Ulster Herald*, February 24, 1990.

[390]Letter from Porter & McCanny to the RUC, January 11, 1991.

[391]Letter from the RUC to Porter & McCanny, July 29, 1994.

[392]Human Rights Watch/Helsinki interview, Limavady, November 21, 1996.

[393]British Irish Rights Watch written submission to the Inquiry into the Killing of Patrick Shanaghan, undated, p. 2. BIRW has also documented many cases in which the RUC warns an individual that his/her security files have been leaked to loyalist paramilitaries or have accidentally gone missing and the RUC advises the person under threat to take necessary security precautions. However, when these same threatened individuals seek home security grants from the Northern Ireland Office to enhance their private security, they are often denied. In addition, the RUC often denies gun permits to the

Constable Ronnie Flanagan dismissed this characterization of the warnings claiming:

> Just because we give warnings doesn't mean there's been some
> lapse in the security system. We don't go into explanations
> because the information often comes from informers.[394]

This explanation avoids the question of how the files were leaked or lost in the first instance. In the absence of any claim or evidence that security procedures were breached, the allegation that a more deliberate scheme has been concocted by security force personnel to pass on classified information to loyalist paramilitaries assumes credibility.

The conduct of RUC officers at the scene of Patrick Shanaghan's murder further calls into question the role of the police in the killing. RUC officers prevented Patrick Shanaghan from receiving medical attention and prohibited a priest from immediate access to him because RUC officers had already pronounced Patrick Shanaghan dead. Dr. W.A. Stewart stated that he was called to the murder scene by the RUC at approximately 8:45 a.m. to attend to a shooting victim.[395] According to Dr. Stewart, when he arrived, "the officer in charge informed me that the victim was dead and instructed me not to proceed as it was his duty to preserve the crime scene."[396] The doctor was advised to return shortly but when he did, he was turned away again. Disturbingly, one witness to the crime scene testified at the inquest that she saw Patrick Shanaghan's head and hands moving after he had been shot.[397] At the inquest, Frank Collins, solicitor for the Shanaghan family, asked the RUC inspector who pronounced Patrick Shanaghan dead if he could have missed a pulse. The inspector replied, "The only way I could have missed a pulse is if the

---

very same individuals it has cautioned about paramilitary threat. See British Irish Rights Watch, *Alleged Collusion and the RUC*, p. 7.

[394]Human Rights Watch/Helsinki interview, Belfast, November 11, 1996.

[395]Written submission of Dr. W.A. Stewart to the Inquiry into the Killing of Patrick Shanaghan, September 1996.

[396]Ibid.

[397]Signed deposition of Delia Margaret Hogg, April 2, 1996.

pulse was so weak it wasn't detectable and a doctor could only detect it."[398] Another physician was called to the murder scene by the RUC at 9:45 a.m. and he pronounced Patrick Shanaghan dead at approximately 9:50 a.m.[399] Despite the fact that the RUC was informed initially that the crime involved a shooting, no ambulance was ever called to the crime scene.

According to Martin Bogues, Patrick Shanaghan's brother-in law, he called Dr. Stewart personally to ask if the doctor had been called to the murder scene. Dr. Stewart told Martin Bogues that he was advised by the RUC to say nothing and that he was also advised not to talk to Mary Shanaghan, Patrick's mother, about what went on that day.[400]

RUC Chief Constable Ronnie Flanagan told Human Rights Watch/Helsinki that he could not comment on the specific details of Patrick Shanaghan's case but it is RUC policy that "only medically qualified people can declare life extinct."[401] He added that there are circumstances where it is obvious that a person is dead and "if there wasn't the remotest prospect of life in existence, an officer's priority would have been preservation of the crime scene."[402] The fact that an eyewitness claimed having seen Patrick Shanaghan move after the shooting and that the RUC inspector admitted he was not qualified to detect a weak pulse, indicate there was a possibility that Patrick Shanaghan was not yet dead when Dr. Stewart arrived at the crime scene at approximately 8:45 a.m. Moreover, since little forensic evidence was gathered at the Shanaghan murder scene and no plaster cast was taken of a tire track found at the scene, it is unclear precisely what the RUC

---

[398]Human Rights Watch/Helsinki telephone conversation with Frank Collins, May 13, 1997.

[399]Written submission of Dr. James Garvey, general practitioner at the Castlederg Health Centre, to the Inquiry into the Killing of Patrick Shanaghan, September 1996.

[400]Human Rights Watch/Helsinki interview, Limavady, November 21, 1996.

[401]Human Rights Watch/Helsinki interview, Belfast, November 24, 1996.

[402]Ibid.

was attempting to preserve when it denied Dr. Stewart access to Patrick Shanaghan. (See section below on the investigation).[403]

Father McGinn, Patrick Shanaghan's parish priest, was also turned away when he arrived at the scene and was directed by two RUC officers to drive to a checkpoint first via an alternative route. Father McGinn estimated that this detour took an additional ten minutes. Patrick Shanaghan was dead when Father McGinn administered last rites at what he estimates was between 9:30 and 9:45 a.m. No explanation was ever given as to why he could not access the crime scene immediately upon his arrival.[404]

The investigation of Patrick Shanaghan's killing appeared to be compromised by RUC incompetency:

- At the time of the shooting, three RUC vehicles were responding to a motor vehicle accident which did not involve injuries. This left no police cars at the station to handle additional calls. When the call to respond to Patrick Shanaghan's shooting came in, only one RUC vehicle, without back up, left the accident scene to attend the murder scene. No ambulance was called to the scene.

- Little forensic evidence was gathered at the crime scene.

---

[403]In July 1996, after she became aware at the inquest of the circumstances surrounding Patrick's death, Mary Shanaghan lodged a series of complaints with the RUC with respect to the conduct of the RUC officers who denied Dr. Stewart access to Patrick and failed to call an ambulance to the scene of the shooting. The complaints, alleging that the RUC's first duty is the preservation of life over the preservation of a crime scene, were forwarded to the Independent Commission for Police Complaints (ICPC). In early 1997, the ICPC informed Mary Shanaghan that the police investigation into her complaints had been completed and the report forwarded to an assistant chief constable who will make a determination as to whether or not disciplinary action or other steps will be taken against the officers involved. Human Rights Watch/Helsinki telephone interview with Martin Bogues, Limavady, May 2, 1997. Copies of the complaints are on file with Human Rights Watch/Helsinki.

[404]Written submission by Father McGinn to the Inquiry into the Killing of Patrick Shanaghan, September 1996.

- Photographs of a tire track at the scene were taken but no plaster cast was made of the track. The RUC claimed that the photos were an adequate substitute for a plaster cast.[405]

- An eyewitness, who saw the shooting from the rearview mirror of his vehicle, was interviewed by an RUC officer only once, immediately after the incident, in an RUC vehicle one-half mile from the crime scene. He was not taken to the scene to describe events as they unfolded nor was he contacted by the RUC again until the inquest was scheduled nearly five years after the killing.[406]

- An RUC mapper made a map of the crime scene but did not take any additional notes. At the inquest, the mapper could not remember why he had marked "xxx" at 44 Learmore Road. It was from the doorway at 44 Learmore Road that the eyewitness claimed to have seen the gunman shoot at Patrick Shanaghan's van.

- The RUC officer who interviewed the eyewitness testified at the inquest that he had no further involvement in the case after the day of the killing until the inquest nearly five years later.

After the family of Patrick Shanaghan was made aware at the inquest of numerous and significant gaps in the murder investigation, it employed an independent forensic science expert to evaluate the quality of the police investigation. Darryl Paul Manners was employed by the Home Office Forensic Science Service for fourteen years, held a Master of Science degree, was a member of the Royal Society of Chemistry and a chartered chemist. Manners' final report concluded that a plaster cast should have been made of the tire print and that the photographs the RUC took were not an adequate substitute for a cast. Manners testified at Patrick Shanaghan's inquest that the photos were "totally unsuitable" for any comparison between the tire imprint and an actual tire to be carried out.[407]

---

[405]Ibid.

[406]This witness stated at the Inquiry into the Killing of Patrick Shanaghan that he was in a state of shock immediately after the incident. Testimony of Raymond Holmes, September 17, 1996.

[407]Signed statement of Daryl Paul Manners, June 3, 1996.

He noted that RUC reliance upon photographs only—particularly photographs not taken "even remotely" to scale and in poor illumination—did not constitute good practice at a crime scene.[408]

The RUC sought judicial review of the coroner's decision to allow Manners' testimony into the inquest record. In the High Court decision, Justice Kerr admitted that he had not read Manners' report but asserted that "how" a person died is to be interpreted narrowly as "by what means" and is not meant "to expose fully those broad circumstances" within which the deceased met his death.[409] Kerr ruled that Manners' report was "evidence in relation to the calibre of the police investigation and went well beyond the scope of the inquiry of the coroner."[410]

The inquest system in Northern Ireland permits for an extremely narrow inquiry.[411] Inquest juries cannot arrive at verdicts as to the responsibility for a death

---

[408]Ibid.

[409]The High Court of Justice in Northern Ireland, *An Application by the Chief Constable of the Royal Ulster Constabulary for Judicial Review in the Matter of Patrick Shanaghan*, KERK2136.T, p. 3.

[410]Ibid.

[411]Coroners rules governing inquests in Northern Ireland are different from those governing inquests in Britain and Wales. The narrow remit and procedural deficits of inquests in Northern Ireland places in question their utility. Inquest juries cannot reach verdicts as to responsibility for a suspicious death. In England and Wales, juries can reach verdicts such as "unlawful killing by an unnamed person." In Northern Ireland, legal aid is not available to families of the deceased although the state funds representation for security force personnel (police and army) and the coroner. There are notoriously long delays in the scheduling of inquests, with some inquest proceedings taking place as much as eight years after a death. Security force personnel suspected of involvement in the death are not compellable witnesses in inquest proceedings and if they do testify their identities can be withheld from the families. The government often issues public interest immunity certificates at the request of the security forces in order to suppress evidence from admission into the record of inquest proceedings. See Helsinki Watch, *Human Rights in Northern Ireland*, pp. 81-84; Committee on the Administration of Justice, *Inquests and Disputed Killings in Northern Ireland* (Belfast: CAJ, January 1992); Tom Hadden, *The Law on Inquests in Northern Ireland: Proposals for Reform*, Paper for Standing Advisory Commission on Human Rights, March 1992. For recent developments in the jurisprudence of inquest procedures, see Jane Winter, "An Overview of the Inquest System," *Just News: Bulletin of the Committee on the Administration of Justice*, July/August 1996, p. 2; and

and may only make conclusions related to the identity of the deceased, and where and how the deceased died. As noted above, the High Court in Northern Ireland has chosen to interpret "how" the deceased died as "by what means," for example, "by gunshot wound," as opposed to under what circumstances. Given these limitations, most "conclusions" reached at inquests contain information that was already known prior to the opening of the inquest.

Patrick Shanaghan's inquest took seven days over three months. Martin Bogues, Patrick's brother-in-law, told Human Rights Watch/Helsinki that from the date of the killing until the inquest commenced, nearly five years later, Patrick's family received no information at all from the RUC. They did not know that an eyewitness had been identified and interviewed nor did they receive any information about an on-going investigation into Patrick's murder. Until the inquest began, they did not know that a tire track had been found at the scene and photographed.   None of Patrick Shanaghan's family members were ever interviewed by the RUC. Although Frank Collins, the Shanaghan family's solicitor, requested all relevant papers from the coroner so the family could prepare for the inquest, he received only the autopsy report and a list of witnesses to be called to testify at the inquest.

The limitations of the inquest system and the successful steps the RUC took to exclude evidence from being entered into the record, led the Shanaghan family and its solicitor to withdraw from the inquest on June 20, 1996. Mary Shanaghan, Patrick's mother, told Human Rights Watch/Helsinki that she decided to withdraw from the inquest after a written statement she submitted to the police in February 1996 for use at the inquest, was edited heavily by the RUC.[412] All references to collusion in Mary Shanaghan's original statement—including her strong belief that the police colluded with the paramilitaries who killed her son— had been excised in the deposition the RUC prepared for the coroner.[413]

Inquests and Contentious Deaths: Record of the Proceedings of a Seminar Held in Belfast on February 1, 1997, sponsored by British Irish Rights Watch, INQUEST, and the Centre for International and Comparative Human Rights Law at the Queen's University of Belfast.

[412]Human Rights Watch/Helsinki interview, Limavady, November 21, 1996.

[413]The February 1996 statement read in part:
It is my belief that collusion between the security forces and paramilitaries was involved in the murder of Patrick. Patrick's death brought to an end a 10 year campaign of continuous harassment against

With one exception, the coroner refused to allow information related to RUC threats against Patrick's life, including Patrick's own signed statements to his solicitors detailing these threats, from being entered into evidence. Much of this information came from Patrick Shanaghan's friends and acquaintances who asserted that death threats against Patrick were passed on to them while they were being interrogated. In some instances, death threats were leveled against individuals after Patrick Shanaghan's murder with RUC detectives using the Shanaghan murder as an example of what could happen to others. The following examples are taken from the transcript of the inquiry:

- Eamonn McGarvey testified that he was interrogated numerous times at Castlereagh holding center: "They made threats against me and made threats about what they were going to do to Paddy, that he hadn't long to live."

- Hugh D'Arcy related a conversation he had with Patrick Shanaghan on October 5, 1990. Patrick said that an RUC officer told him that the police would not be picking him up anymore because Patrick would be "going to the graveyard on the hill."

- Paddy O'Donnell testified that about five weeks before Patrick Shanaghan's murder, five uniformed RUC officers came to his home and told O'Donnell that he would "end up being shot" if he continued to keep company with Patrick Shanaghan.

- Kevin McMenamin said that he and Patrick Shanaghan were both being interrogated at Castlereagh in May 1991 when an RUC officer told him that Patrick "would never see his next birthday and the van won't be going up to the big house on the hill too often."

---

him. This included 16 house searches when our home was ransacked and damaged, 10 periods of detention without charge, death threats made by detectives at Castlereagh Holding Centre and the leaking of his security file to loyalist paramilitaries. His daily life was one of constant road blocks, searches, insults and threats from the security forces.

None of this language appeared in the coroner's deposition. Copies of both the original statement and the edited deposition are on file with Human Rights Watch/Helsinki.

- Packie Kelly told the Inquiry that when he was detained in Castlereagh in July 1992, the RUC "put heavy emphasis on the Shanaghan killing saying that they had got him sorted out and that the same people were going to be put at myself. They said they got the UV's [Ulster Volunteers] to sort him out."

- John Corry testified that he was detained at Castlereagh from May 20-22, 1992. During one interrogation, an RUC officer shouted at him, "You know what happened to Patrick Shanaghan, the bastard, don't you? He didn't walk out in front of a car and was killed. Don't forget that at long last the Prods have got their act together around Castlederg."[414]

- Damien Harper submitted a written statement to Patrick Shanaghan's solicitors, Porter and McCanny, which alleged that while being interrogated at Castlereagh in March 1995, an RUC detective told Harper that "Patrick Shanaghan was threatened in that same chair and the same will happen to you when you leave here." The detective told Harper that he would have Harper shot "the same as Patrick Shanaghan."

The coroner, however, decided to permit David Cameron, a friend of Patrick Shanaghan's, to give testimony at the inquest based on a statement Cameron originally gave to his solicitor which was then turned over to Frank Collins, the Shanaghan family's solicitor, for use at Patrick Shanaghan's inquest. The statement read:

> In January 1991 Patrick Shanaghan informed me that while he was being held in Castlereagh...he was informed by one of his interrogators that this was going to be the year of Shanaghan and Cameron. Then on May 14, 1991, I was arrested at my home and taken to Castlereagh...and was told during one interview that Paddy Shanaghan and I was responsible for all the terrorist activities in the Castlederg area and we was going to be taken

---

[414]"Prods" is a derogatory term used to describe Protestants.

out. I was told our names would be leaked to [John Doe] who has connections with the UDA.[415]

The RUC sought judicial review of the Coroner's decision to allow Cameron to testify. The High Court held in favor of the RUC and ruled that David Cameron would not be permitted to give evidence because it

> is not germane to the question which the Coroner and the jury must decide and that is by what means the deceased met his death. Evidence has already been given without apparent challenge that the deceased was the target of loyalist terrorists before he was murdered. That evidence has not been disputed and is no way controversial and in those circumstances it appears to me that the only issue which Mr. Cameron's evidence could shed light upon is whether these threats were uttered by police officers. That, for the reasons I have already referred to, is not a matter for the Coroner's inquest to enquire into. . .[416]

The same day the Shanaghan family withdrew from the inquest, a "Verdict on Inquest" was issued stating that Patrick Shanaghan died on August 12, 1991, on Learmore Road in Castlederg, County Tyrone, from a bullet wound to his chest.[417]

As noted above, RUC Chief Constable Ronnie Flanagan, declined to comment on the details of the investigation into Patrick Shanaghan's case. When asked whether he considered the Shanaghan murder an "open" case, Flanagan told

---

[415]Deposition of David Cameron, April 23, 1996. The name "John Doe" has been substituted for the name of the man with paramilitary connections to whom the RUC was threatening to turn over information about David Cameron and Patrick Shanaghan.

[416]The High Court of Northern Ireland, *An Application by the Chief Constable of the Royal Ulster Constabulary for Judicial Review in the Matter of Patrick Shanaghan,* KERK2136.T, pp. 3-4.

[417]Coroners Act (Northern Ireland) 1959, Verdict on Inquest Touching the Death of Patrick Sean (sic) Shanaghan, dated 20th June 1996. (Patrick Shanaghan's middle name is "John" but appeared as "Sean" on all court papers despite requests by the Shanaghan family solicitor for the insertion of the deceased's proper name in all official documents.)

Human Rights Watch/Helsinki: "I consider open every case which has not culminated in a person going through the criminal process."[418]

Human Rights Watch/Helsinki calls on the RUC to inform the Shanaghan family that the investigation of the murder of Patrick Shanaghan remains open and to provide the family and its solicitor with a detailed report on the progress of the investigation, taking into consideration confidential information that may compromise the eventual apprehension of a suspect. We urge that any ongoing investigation conform to the United Nations Principles on the Effective Prevention and Investigation of Extra-Legal, Arbitrary and Summary Executions requiring a "thorough, prompt and impartial investigation" of all suspected cases of arbitrary execution.[419] In compliance with the U.N. Principles, we strongly urge the chief constable to investigate vigorously allegations that certain RUC officers made death threats against Patrick Shanaghan and threatened to, or actually did, leak his security information to loyalist paramilitaries. The U.N. Principles state:

> 3. Governments shall prohibit orders from superior officers or public authorities authorizing or inciting other persons to carry out any such extra-legal or summary executions.

> 4. Effective protection through judicial or other means shall be guaranteed to individuals and groups who are in danger of extra-legal, arbitrary or summary executions, including those who receive death threats.

> 18. Governments shall ensure that persons identified by the investigation as having participated in extra-legal, arbitrary or summary executions in any territory under their jurisdiction are brought to justice.[420]

---

[418]Human Rights Watch/Helsinki interview, Belfast, November 24, 1996.

[419]United Nations Principles on the Effective Prevention and Investigation of Extra-Legal, Arbitrary and Summary Executions, E.S.C. res. 1989/65, annex, 1989 U.N. ESCOR Supp. (No. 1) at 52, U.N. Doc. E/1989/89 (1989). In resolution 1989/65, paragraph 1, ECOSOC recommended that these principles be taken into account and respected by governments within the framework of their national legislation and practices. See Appendix I.

[420]Ibid.

In addition, Human Rights Watch/Helsinki recommends in the strongest terms possible that the government of the United Kingdom take all necessary steps to halt the type of collusion well-documented in the Stevens Inquiry and strongly suggested by the murder of Patrick Shanaghan.

The Case of Colin Duffy

On January 2, 1990, three republicans, Colin Duffy, Tony McCaughey and Samuel Marshall were arrested for possessing illegal weapons.[421] The three men were at the home of Frances McCaughey, Marshall's sister, when RUC officers entered and reportedly discovered ten rounds of .445 ammunition in the toilet bowl. Samuel Marshall and Colin Duffy were released on February 1, 1990, on bail arrangements requiring the men to report to the Lurgan RUC station every Wednesday evening at 7:30 p.m. and Saturday afternoons at 2:30 p.m. to sign a bail book. The bail arrangements were not made public and were known only to the two men, their solicitors, and the RUC. On March 2, 1990, Tony McCaughey was granted bail with the same reporting requirements.

After the release of Marshall and Duffy, a Portadown RUC station detective received a telephone call in the name of a loyalist paramilitary group threatening Samuel Marshall and a number of other republicans with death. RUC Special Branch assessed the threat, determined that it was serious, and made a report to the subdivisional commander at Lurgan RUC station on February 13, 1990. Two weeks later, an RUC inspector informed Samuel Marshall's mother that her son was under paramilitary threat.

On Wednesday, March 7, 1990, at 7:40 p.m., Samuel Marshall was shot dead by two masked men at an intersection near the Lurgan RUC station where he, Colin Duffy and Tony McCaughey had just signed the bail book. Colin Duffy and Tony McCaughey escaped. The next day, Colin Duffy and Tony McCaughey were interviewed at the Lurgan RUC station in the presence of their solicitor. The men gave an account of the events surrounding Samuel Marshall's death and alleged that they had been under constant surveillance from the time they started signing for bail. On March 9, 1990, they participated in a Sinn Féin press conference accusing the RUC of colluding with Marshall's killers. At the press conference, they detailed the factors which led them to make the collusion charge:

---

[421]Human Rights Watch/Helsinki relied heavily on British Irish Rights Watch's, *Allegations of Collusion and the RUC*, pp. 11-16, for details of Samuel Marshall's murder. BIRW's account is taken from two primary sources: an RUC report submitted by Detective/Investigator Alan Clegg and the transcript of Clegg's cross-examination at an extradition trial in California in November 1993.

- The men had observed a red Maestro car on three separate occasions on the way to the RUC station the evening Samuel Marshall was killed. The men had seen the car in that area twice before and assumed it was a police surveillance vehicle keeping tabs on them. (It was later confirmed by the RUC to have been a surveillance vehicle.)

- A sangar [sentry post] at the front of the RUC station normally unattended at night due to the security risk, was occupied by two men the evening Samuel Marshall was killed. Only the heads of the men in the sangar could be seen and they were not wearing RUC caps. Duffy and McCaughey alleged that the men were keeping them under surveillance and were in radio contact with the red Maestro.

- Duffy and McCaughey also noticed another car, a red Rover, which passed them twice after they and Samuel Marshall had left the RUC station. According to Tony McCaughey, the Rover stopped just below the intersection where Samuel Marshall was killed.

According to Duffy and McCaughey, there was a link between the red Maestro, the Rover driven by paramilitaries, and the men in the sangar.

Colin Duffy told Human Rights Watch/Helsinki that a week after the first press conference, sophisticated surveillance equipment—a camera directed toward his house—was found close to his home.[422] Sinn Féin called another press conference after the discovery of this equipment and once again Colin Duffy publicly questioned the role of the RUC in both the death of Samuel Marshall and the attempt on Duffy's own life.

Despite RUC denials of collusion, several subsequent developments fueled Duffy's claims of security force involvement in Samuel Marshall's murder:

- While testifying under oath at an extradition trial in the U.S., RUC Inspector Alan Clegg admitted that the red Maestro was on a surveillance mission but claimed Samuel Marshall was not the mission's target nor was the Maestro a police car.[423]

---

[422]Human Rights Watch/Helsinki interview, Belfast, November 19, 1996.

[423]British Irish Rights Watch counts Clegg's testimony as strong evidence that the car was an MI5 (military intelligence) vehicle. *Alleged Collusion and the RUC*, p. 15.

•   The Rover McCaughey saw the night Marshall was killed was hijacked
         by two members of the UVF on March 6, 1993. It was found burning by
         the side of a motorway the night Samuel Marshall was killed. Although
         the UFF ultimately claimed responsibility for the murder, it was a UVF
         member, Victor Graham, who helped hijack the car and was subsequently
         convicted of aiding and abetting the murder of Samuel Marshall. The
         Rover was determined to have been used in the murder. The other UVF
         member, Raymond Falls, was convicted of hijacking.

•   The presence of the two men in the RUC sangar the night Samuel
         Marshall was killed was never explained.

The coroner decided not to hold an inquest into Samuel Marshall's death
because he contended that all the relevant facts concerning the death had been
established at the trial of Graham and Falls. This is misleading as Graham was
convicted for "aiding and abetting" and Falls was convicted for hijacking. Clearly,
the relevant facts concerning the death of Samuel Marshall have yet to be
determined. No one has ever been charged with the murder of Samuel Marshall.
        When Human Rights Watch/Helsinki interviewed Colin Duffy in
November 1996, he had been acquitted recently of the murder of John Lyness, a
former Ulster Defense Regiment/Royal Irish Regiment sergeant. Duffy told us he
believed the RUC set him up for Lyness' murder because he had publicly accused
the RUC of collusion in the murder of Samuel Marshall.[424] The circumstances of
Duffy's conviction—and acquittal on appeal—for Lyness' murder, at the very least
raise troubling questions about RUC policy and practice with respect to securing
witness testimony. At worst, RUC conduct in Colin Duffy's case can only serve to
fuel allegations of official collusion between loyalist paramilitary groups and the
police.
        According to Colin Duffy, he was constantly harassed by the RUC
between 1990 and June 24, 1993, the date of John Lyness' murder:

            Between 1990 and 1993, my house was searched six or eight
            times. I have a wife and child. They never found anything. There
            were never any charges. I was lifted four or five times. On the
            street, I was stopped and p-checked. Searched. If the child was
            with me, she was searched. They [the RUC] don't have to say
            anything. They know your face. They ask you your name,

---

[424]Human Rights Watch/Helsinki interview, Belfast, November 19, 1996.

where you're going. If it's winter, they try to get you to take your coat off or your shoes off. Any time they seen me, they stopped me.[425]

John Lyness was shot and killed near his home at Lime Grove, Lurgan, County Portadown. An intense security operation followed the killing during which many homes in the area were searched, including Colin Duffy's. The Duffy family was not home at the time of the search and decided to stay at Duffy's mother-in-law's house the day immediately after the murder because "the area was saturated with RUC."[426] On June 28, 1993, Colin Duffy was arrested in connection with the murder of John Lyness at the Crumlin Road Court House in Belfast where he had been attending a trial.

Colin Duffy was taken to Gough Barracks for interrogation. He requested counsel immediately and was not interrogated until he had conferred with his solicitor, Rosemary Nelson, who he said advised him not to answer any questions.[427] Duffy, who was to deny any involvement in the murder, reportedly was advised not to offer an alibi because it would probably result in the arrest of family members, including Duffy's wife and elderly mother-in-law.[428] Colin Duffy described his interrogations to Human Rights Watch/Helsinki:

> They weren't telling me anything at all. I'm remaining silent. They were writing questions on a paper: "Did you kill John Lyness? No reply." They didn't *ask* me any questions. They didn't defer my solicitor knowing that I didn't have any information to give her so she could advise me. I didn't get any information that first night to give Rosemary any information so she could properly advise me. It's a way around the deferral.[429]

---

[425]Human Rights Watch/Helsinki interview, Belfast, November 19, 1996.

[426]Ibid.

[427]Human Rights Watch interview, Belfast, November 19, 1996.

[428]Ibid.

[429]Under the Northern Ireland (Emergency Provisions) Act section 47, access to counsel may be deferred for the first forty-eight hours of detention. (See chapter one "Policing Northern Ireland" for a discussion of the emergency legislation in force in

The next morning, I told Rosemary I sensed something was going on because they didn't allow me to read the notes. . .In the interview again, they put it to me that I was the one who killed John Lyness. I made denials. From Monday through Thursday, I made approximately thirty-six denials. I got no other information.[430]

Duffy was charged with the murder of John Lyness on July 1, 1993, but his trial did not commence until May 1995, after he had served nearly two years on remand. At a special court session on July 2, 1993, Rosemary Nelson discovered that the evidence against Colin Duffy consisted of one eyewitness referred to by the letter "B." Nelson assumed the letter designation meant the witness was a member of the security forces although when she asked the RUC officer in charge of the investigation if this was so, he refused to answer.[431] Witness B's statement claimed that he had been driving twenty meters from the murder scene and never stopped his vehicle but saw two gunmen at the scene. He stated that he had only a side view of the man who shot John Lyness but was certain that the gunman was Colin Duffy.[432] It was discovered subsequently that Witness B was a member of the Royal Irish Regiment.

At a preliminary inquiry held in late 1993, a surprise statement from another witness given the letter designation "C" was entered into evidence by the Crown. Rosemary Nelson told Human Rights Watch/Helsinki that "the statement was dated July 23, 1993, and the event [Lyness' murder] happened on June 24, 1993. It had been fairly well publicized that Colin Duffy had been charged."[433] Witness C claimed to have been walking in Lurgan Park the evening of the murder and to have seen two men on bicycles cross his path. He unequivocally identified Colin Duffy as one of the men. Witness C made the identification based on his recollection of seeing Duffy for the first time nine years prior to Lyness' shooting

---

Northern Ireland.)

[430]Human Rights Watch/Helsinki interview, Belfast, November 19, 1996.

[431]Human Rights Watch/Helsinki interview, Belfast, November 19, 1996.

[432]Belfast Crown Court, *Regina v. Colin Duffy,* Trial Transcript, p. 16.

[433]Human Rights Watch/Helsinki interview, Belfast, November 19, 1996.

in a public house.[434] Witness C indicated that he also saw Duffy three or four years before the murder in that same public house.[435]

Colin Duffy's trial was scheduled for November 14, 1994. Rosemary Nelson was informed by the Crown two days before trial that three boxes of information were available for examination by the defense. She requested an adjournment to prepare an adequate defense. The information in the trial documents revealed that another eyewitness designated "A" had provided the Crown with a full description of the two men at the murder scene. Despite being shown a photo lineup which included a photograph of Colin Duffy, witness A failed to identify Duffy as one of the men he had seen on June 24, 1993.[436] Rosemary Nelson told Human Rights Watch/Helsinki she was not informed that Colin Duffy's photograph was being used for identification purposes and that a live identification parade was the proper method for the identification of suspects.[437] There was no information at all in the boxes about witness C.

Colin Duffy's trial commenced in May 1995 with Mr. Justice Kerr presiding. Although witnesses A and B testified from behind a screen, their identities were revealed to the judge, Crown prosecutors and the defense. According to Rosemary Nelson, however, "the Crown made every effort to conceal witness C's identity."[438] These efforts included an *ex parte* application to an outside judge, Mr. Justice Campbell, for permission to withhold witness C's identity from the trial judge and the defense. The application was denied and the trial adjourned for two days so the defense could investigate witness C, Lindsay Robb. It transpired that Robb was a member of the Progressive Unionist Party (PUP) delegation to the Stormont talks.[439] It is widely believed that the PUP is

---

[434]*Regina v. Colin Duffy*, p. 24

[435]Ibid.

[436]Ibid., p. 9.

[437]Human Rights Watch/Helsinki interview, Belfast, November 19, 1996.

[438]Ibid.

[439]These preliminary peace talks involved all the political parties in Northern Ireland, with the exception of Sinn Féin. The talks at the time focused on arriving at an agreement for the decommissioning of paramilitary weapons and setting an agenda for the commencement of peace negotiations. Sinn Féin was excluded because the party refused

associated with the outlawed loyalist paramilitary group, the UVF, and that the party represents the interests of the UVF at the negotiating table. Rosemary Nelson told Human Rights Watch/Helsinki that she found out about Robb, "completely by accident" after she read an interview he had given to a local newspaper, *The Lurgan Mail*, about his political activities.[440] An investigation into Robb's background revealed that he was the only member of the PUP delegation with no record for the commission of terrorist crimes. The RUC told defense investigators that Robb was a good family man.[441]

At trial, Robb was cross-examined about links between the PUP and the UVF. He strongly denied knowledge of any link between the party and the paramilitary organization claiming that he did not personally know certain UVF leaders and that he condemned violence.[442] He remained firm, however, in his identification of Colin Duffy, despite testifying that neither of the cyclists he had seen on June 24, 1993, looked directly at him nor could he describe what they were wearing.

Colin Duffy was convicted for the murder of John Lyness in July 1995 and sentenced to life in prison. In his judgment, Justice Kerr dismissed any inconsistencies in witness B's testimony and accepted that he had recognized Colin Duffy.[443] Although Colin Duffy detailed his movements on the day of the murder in his trial testimony, thus providing an alibi, the judge drew adverse inferences from Duffy's refusal to offer an alibi during interrogation at Gough Barracks. The judge disregarded Duffy's explanation at trial that he feared family members might be arrested and interrogated if he gave alibi evidence.[444]

Significantly, Justice Kerr relied heavily on the testimony of witness C in convicting Colin Duffy. The judge commended witness C for his candor and reliability and observed that intense cross-examination of the witness by the

---

to agree to the surrender of IRA weapons as a precondition to joining the talks. (See Introduction of this report.)

[440]Human Rights Watch/Helsinki interview, Belfast, November 19, 1996.

[441]Ibid.

[442]Ibid.

[443]*Regina v. Colin Duffy*, p. 60.

[444]Ibid., p. 69.

defense served to present witness C as a man of "obvious honesty."[445] Justice Kerr described witness C as "convincing in his explanation of his political beliefs and the impartiality of his testimony" and, as a witness alleged by the defense to be incapable of objectivity due to his views on the situation in Northern Ireland, "his evidence on this and all other aspects of the case have been the hallmarks of accuracy and honesty."[446] Colin Duffy appealed immediately.

Within weeks of Colin Duffy's conviction, Lindsay Robb was arrested in Scotland and charged with attempting to procure arms for the UVF and with possession of illegal arms. It transpired that Robb was the object of a prolonged surveillance operation jointly conducted by British military intelligence and a number of United Kingdom police forces, including the RUC. According to press reports, the operation's purpose was to crack down on hardliners in the UVF who threatened to break the loyalist paramilitary cease fire.[447] Allegedly, the security forces in Northern Ireland were ordered to keep the UVF and Robb under close scrutiny.[448] A senior RUC intelligence officer testified at Robb's trial that the UVF continued to gather arms: "Intelligence would indicate they are still going about their business, although there's no violence whatsoever."[449] British military intelligence officers also testified about the details of the surveillance operation at Robb's trial.[450]

An RUC sergeant testified at Robb's trial that after Colin Duffy was convicted in July 1995, the RUC gave Lindsay Robb £2,000 to move to Scotland and a gun for his protection.[451] This put the RUC in the untenable position of surveilling Robb for involvement in paramilitary activities at the same time it used Robb as a witness—allegedly with no paramilitary contacts—in Colin Duffy's trial.

---

[445]Ibid., p. 48.

[446]Ibid.

[447]Severin Carrell, "Loyalists Guilty in Arms Case," *The Scotsman*, December 7, 1995.

[448]Ibid.

[449]"UVF Ready for Action, Court Told," *The Herald*, December 1, 1995.

[450]"MI5 Agents Tell of Following Loyalists," *The Herald*, November 23, 1995.

[451]"Terrorism Accused was Given a New Life," *The Herald*, December 5, 1995.

Lindsay Robb was convicted on the arms charges in December 1995 and sentenced to ten years in prison.

The defense actively sought discovery of Lindsay Robb's indictment and the transcript from Robb's trial for use in Colin Duffy's appeal. In July 1996, the Crown informed Rosemary Nelson that it no longer intended to rely on witness C's evidence because "subsequent events showed him to be an 'unreliable witness.'"[452] The Appeals Court stated that "after Lindsay Robb was convicted of a terrorist offence and that conviction showed his evidence at trial about his own activities to be completely untrue, . . .[t]his cast grave doubt upon the reliability and truthfulness of the evidence which he had given."[453]

Colin Duffy was acquitted in September 1996 after the appeal judge determined that witness B's evidence alone could not be relied upon.

RUC Chief Constable Ronnie Flanagan declined to comment on the details of Colin Duffy's case due to an ongoing civil action lodged by Duffy. Flanagan did offer a general statement with respect to RUC policy and witness protection:

> There is nothing unusual with protecting witnesses. If a witness is willing to give evidence to the Crown, we have an obligation to protect them. If we are protecting a witness we must disclose that so that the Crown is not seen as buying a witness.[454]

Rosemary Nelson told Human Rights Watch/Helsinki:

> Lindsay Robb was dishonest. He denied any knowledge of the UVF. The RUC knew about his ties to paramilitary groups and yet they gave him money and a safe house.[455]

---

[452]Ibid.

[453]Court of Appeal of Northern Ireland, *The Queen v. Colin Francis Duffy*, HUTE2200, p. 2.

[454]Human Rights Watch/Helsinki interview, Belfast, November 24, 1996.

[455]Human Rights Watch/Helsinki interview, Belfast, November 19, 1996.

The Case of Rosemary Nelson

Rosemary Nelson's representation of Colin Duffy resulted in a pattern of intimidation against both her and her clients in the aftermath of Duffy's acquittal. The intimidation of defense lawyers by the RUC has been well-documented,[456] but the nature of the threats recently leveled against Rosemary Nelson, especially in light of Colin Duffy's acquittal, have made her fear that some sort of reprisal is imminent. Rosemary Nelson reported that over a three to four week period in early 1997, twelve of her clients who had been arrested came out of detention at Gough Barracks in Armagh saying that RUC officers had threatened that she was going to be killed:

> When they [clients] requested me, immediately things were said about me, "she's a terrorist, that makes you a terrorist." RUC detectives were making these statements. Any time that I arrived down, any time the clients were told I was there, they would say, "she's an IRA woman, she's going to be shot" or "she's going to be taken out soon." They also said that I was down there supplying sex to my clients or I must be good in bed and that is why they were requesting me. It's so demeaning, it's incredible. It's difficult to face a client when they're making comments like that. You can usually tolerate it, but it got too heavy. There's one particular RUC officer there who was involved with the Duffy case in relation to the prosecution and he detests me. He's one of the officers making these threats.[457]

Two of Rosemary Nelson's clients offered written accounts of the threats leveled against them, Colin Duffy, and Rosemary Nelson:[458]

> **Client #1:** They asked, "What's Rosemary telling you?". . . They said I got the wrong advice—look at how many people she

---

[456]British-Irish Rights Watch, *Report to the United Nations Special Rapporteur on the Independence of Judges and Lawyers* (London: BIRW, December 1996); Lawyers Committee for Human Rights, *Human Rights and Legal Defense in Northern Ireland*, 1993 and *At the Crossroads*, 1996.

[457]Human Rights Watch/Helsinki telephone interview, March 7, 1997.

[458]Copies of these statements are on file with Human Rights Watch/Helsinki.

put away. They said she was the one who touted and I'm going to be shot. They put my family under threat, they said, "we'll shoot all of you." They went out of the room and came back in and said, "he's hiding something, we need to get it out of him, the fine bastard. You're dead. Tell Rosemary she's going to die, too." They threatened to pass my photo and details to loyalists.

Client #2: They said, "You're a target, your family's a target. The last person I said that to is in a wooden box." . . .They said, "You're number five down in the estate. Colin Duffy's number one." They . . . said they would get Colin Duffy. They said they would do whatever it took to get rid of "you Provo bastards." They said they would give details to loyalists. They said [Rosemary] was a friend of the Provos and of Colin Duffy's. They said, "she's not that good, she won't get you off."

Rosemary Nelson has lodged a complaint with the RUC concerning the death threats and the inappropriate sexual innuendos made against her.

Despite well-documented claims of threats and harassment of defense lawyers, neither the Law Society of Northern Ireland nor the Bar Council of Northern Ireland have publicly campaigned against lawyer intimidation. Michael Davey, secretary of the Law Society, the professional association of solicitors, stated that the society is against lawyer intimidation, "but there has been no request for the Law Society to take any action with respect to it."[459] Davey added that intimidation is used as an interrogation tool by police forces all over the world. Richard Montieth, chairperson of the Law Society's Human Rights Committee, told Human Rights Watch/Helsinki that "intimidation happens to Protestant solicitors as well as Catholic solicitors. Any defense lawyer is liable to opprobrious comments."[460] Eugene Grant, chairman of the Bar Council of Northern Ireland,

---

[459]Human Rights watch/Helsinki interview, Belfast, November 14, 1996. This claim is astonishing in light of the murder of Patrick Finucane. The Law Society itself never publicly condemned Finucane's murder. The day after the murder, the president of the Law Society—in his personal capacity—issued a statement condemning the murder. Even if no individual member of the Law Society requested specific action by the society in the aftermath of the murder, it is surely within the power of the society's executive to condemn the paramilitary assassination of one of its members.

[460]Ibid.

which represents barristers, told us that while "solicitors are under attack, . . . they withstand the vilification. Solicitors are extremely strong in dealing with intimidation. They get on with it. The intimidation of solicitors has no great effect on the justice system; clients don't lose any confidence."[461]

While it is true that criminal defense lawyers worldwide are subject to contemptuous responses from law enforcement officials, death threats against lawyers in Northern Ireland—particularly since the murder of Patrick Finucane in 1989—raise the stakes significantly for those lawyers under threat. By casting the intimidation of defense lawyers merely as an occupational hazard, the Law Society and Bar Council fail in their responsibility to assist members of the legal profession to counsel their clients without undue interference from state authorities.[462]

Human Rights Watch/Helsinki calls on the RUC to investigate adequately Rosemary Nelson's claims of lawyer intimidation. We also urge the government of the United Kingdom to take measures to ensure the independence of lawyers so that they can carry out their duties without undue interference from law enforcement officials. Furthermore, we encourage the Bar Council and Law Society of Northern Ireland to advocate on behalf of and support efforts to change the current ethos of threat and degradation that characterizes the practice of criminal defense work in Northern Ireland.

Relatives Groups

Relatives of victims of loyalist paramilitary killings have organized groups in Northern Ireland whose purpose is to bring attention to the issue of collusion. Relatives for Justice, a group of relatives representing those killed by the security forces in Northern Ireland, compiled a list of loyalist paramilitary killings beginning with the murder of Samuel Marshall in 1990 to the murder of John O'Hanlon in North Belfast on September 1, 1994.[463] O'Hanlon was the last victim

---

[461]Human Rights Watch/Helsinki interview, Belfast, November 6, 1996.

[462]United Nations Basic Principles on the Role of Lawyers, Eighth United Nations Congress on the Prevention of Crime and the Treatment of Offenders, Havana Cuba, 27 August to 7 September 1990, U.N. Doc. A/CONF.144/28/Rev.1 at 118 (1990). Principle 25 requires professional associations to ensure that "lawyers are able, without improper interference to counsel and assist their clients in accordance with the law and recognized professional standards and ethics."

[463]Relatives for Justice, *Collusion 1990-1994* (Belfast: Relatives for Justice, 1995), p. 1.

of loyalist violence before loyalist paramilitaries declared a cease fire on October 13, 1994. In *Collusion 1990-1994: Loyalist Paramilitary Murders in North of Ireland*, Relatives for Justice outlined its concerns and documented how factors suggesting collusion are a routine feature of loyalist paramilitary killings. A sample of the group's concerns includes:

- **Security intelligence files continue to be leaked.** Samples of newspaper reports from June 1990 to August 1994 indicate that security files containing photo montages and personal details of nationalists frequently go missing. Relatives for Justice documents twenty-five news accounts of RUC warnings of loyalist paramilitary threat due to information contained in such "missing" files.

- **Security force response to nationalist appeals for adequate protection go unheeded.** Noting that loyalist paramilitaries use the same routes in and out of nationalist communities when they attack, Relatives for Justice questions both the lack of response to calls for better security on those routes and the apparent failure of the British army and RUC to employ such sophisticated surveillance equipment to counter incursions by loyalist paramilitaries.

- **Security forces often direct oppressive follow-up operations at nationalist communities.** In the aftermath of loyalist paramilitary killings, security forces establish check points, harass residents, and disrupt wakes and funerals in the community in which the victim resided.

- **Security force forensic teams often fail to employ good forensic practices.** Forensic material—for example, bullets used in a loyalist paramilitary attack—is often left at the scene. The RUC has also refused to disclose the ballistic history of weapons used in such killings.

Martin Finucane, brother of Patrick Finucane and a spokesperson for Relatives for Justice, told Human Rights Watch/Helsinki:

> We see the dirty war that's being carried on here and we have a
> right to know the details of human rights violations. Collusion
> has caused an ethos of impunity within the security forces. The

RUC has the perception that they wouldn't be prosecuted for wrongdoing.[464]

Human Rights Watch/Helsinki met with another relatives group during its November 1996 mission. The group consists of over thirty families who have had relatives murdered by a loyalist paramilitary organization. Although many relatives believe that collusion between the RUC and the loyalist paramilitaries was a core feature of the killings, members of this group were reluctant to state so publicly and many members requested anonymity from Human Rights Watch/Helsinki.[465] Every group member with whom we spoke gave detailed evidence of factors suggesting collusion in the killings of their family members. Despite this evidence, the group's strategy is to bring pressure to bear on the RUC to bring charges against those responsible. To date, there have been few convictions for the murders of the nearly forty victims which the group represents. The murder investigations generally have been inadequate and/or incompetent. Most members of the group were never interviewed by the RUC after the murders. Family members report that they have been intimidated or harassed by the security forces since the murders. Inquests have been held in almost all the cases—in some cases, years after the murder— but many relatives did not understand the nature of the proceedings or their right to be represented by counsel, call witnesses, and make statements. One inquest lasted fifteen minutes.

---

[464]Human Rights Watch/Helsinki interview, London/Derry, November 23, 1996.

[465]Given the high degree of fear of loyalist paramilitary retribution expressed by this group, Human Rights Watch/Helsinki has decided not to include any identification information with respect to this meeting. We detail some of our impressions in order to highlight the fact that allegations of collusion are not limited to a few high profile cases but effect a much larger group of people. We also include a profile of this meeting to illustrate how difficult it is to investigate allegations of collusion in Northern Ireland and how dangerous publicizing such allegations can be to the families involved.

APPENDIX: Principles on the Effective Prevention and Investigation of Extra-Legal, Arbitrary and Summary Executions[466]

Prevention

1. Governments shall prohibit by law all extra-legal, arbitrary and summary executions and shall ensure that any such executions are recognized as offences under their criminal laws, and are punishable by appropriate penalties which take into account the seriousness of such offences. Exceptional circumstances including a state of war or threat of war, internal political instability or any other public emergency may not be invoked as a justification of such executions. Such executions shall not be carried out under any circumstances including, but not limited to, situations of internal armed conflict, excessive or illegal use of force by a public official or other person acting in an official capacity or by a person acting at the instigation, or with the consent or acquiescence of such person, and situations in which deaths occur in custody. This prohibition shall prevail over decrees issued by governmental authority.

2. In order to prevent extra-legal, arbitrary and summary executions, Governments shall ensure strict control, including a clear chain of command over all officials responsible for apprehension, arrest, detention, custody and imprisonment, as well as those officials authorized by law to use force and firearms.

3. Governments shall prohibit orders from superior officers or public authorities authorizing or inciting other persons to carry out any such extralegal, arbitrary or summary executions. All persons shall have the right and the duty to defy such orders. Training of law enforcement officials shall emphasize the above provisions.

4. Effective protection through judicial or other means shall be guaranteed to individuals and groups who are in danger of extra-legal, arbitrary or summary executions, including those who receive death threats.

5. No one shall be involuntarily returned or extradited to a country where there are substantial grounds for believing that he or she may become a victim of extra-legal, arbitrary or summary execution in that country.

6. Governments shall ensure that persons deprived of their liberty are held in officially recognized places of custody, and that accurate information on their custody and whereabouts, including transfers, is made promptly available to their relatives and lawyer or other persons of confidence.

---

[466] E.S.C. res. 1989/65, annex, 1989 U.N. ESCOR Supp. (No. 1) at 52, U.N. Doc. E/1989/89 (1989).

7. Qualified inspectors, including medical personnel, or an equivalent independent authority, shall conduct inspections in places of custody on a regular basis, and be empowered to undertake unannounced inspections on their own initiative, with full guarantees of independence in the exercise of this function. The inspectors shall have unrestricted access to all persons in such places of custody, as well as to all their records.

8. Governments shall make every effort to prevent extra-legal, arbitrary and summary executions through measures such as diplomatic intersession, improved access of complainants to intergovernmental and judicial bodies, and public denunciation. Intergovernmental mechanisms shall be used to investigate reports of any such executions and to take effective action against such practices. Governments, including those of countries where extra-legal, arbitrary and summary executions are reasonably suspected to occur, shall cooperate fully in international investigations on the subject.

Investigation

9. There shall be thorough, prompt and impartial investigation of all suspected cases of extra-legal, arbitrary and summary executions, including eases where complaints by relatives or other reliable reports suggest unnatural death in the above circumstances. Governments shall maintain investigative offices and procedures to undertake such inquiries. The purpose of the investigation shall be to determine the cause, manner and time of death, the person responsible, and any pattern or practice which may have brought about that death. It shall include an adequate autopsy, collection and analysis of all physical and documentary evidence and statements from witnesses. The investigation shall distinguish between natural death, accidental death, suicide and homicide.

10. The investigative authority shall have the power to obtain all the information necessary to the inquiry. Those persons conducting the investigation shall have at their disposal all the necessary budgetary and technical resources for effective investigation. They shall also have the authority to oblige officials allegedly involved in any such executions to appear and testify. The same shall apply to any witness. To this end, they shall be entitled to issue summonses to witnesses, including the officials allegedly involved and to demand the production of evidence.

11. In cases in which the established investigative procedures are inadequate because of lack of expertise or impartiality, because of the importance of the matter or because of the apparent existence of a pattern of abuse, and in cases where there are complaints from the family of the victim about these inadequacies or other substantial reasons, Governments shall pursue investigations

through an independent commission of inquiry or similar procedure. Members of such a commission shall be chosen for their recognized impartiality, competence and independence as individuals. In particular, they shall be independent of any institution, agency or person that may be the subject of the inquiry. The commission shall have the authority to obtain all information necessary to the inquiry and shall conduct the inquiry as provided for under these Principles.

12. The body of the deceased person shall not be disposed of until an adequate autopsy is conducted by a physician, who shall, if possible, be an expert in forensic pathology. Those conducting the autopsy shall have the right of access to all investigative data, to the place where the body was discovered, and to the place where the death is thought to have occurred. If the body has been buried and it later appears that an investigation is required, the body shall be promptly and competently exhumed for an autopsy. If skeletal remains are discovered, they should be carefully exhumed and studied according to systematic anthropological techniques.

13. The body of the deceased shall be available to those conducting the autopsy for a sufficient amount of time to enable a thorough investigation to be carried out. The autopsy shall, at a minimum, attempt to establish the identity of the deceased and the cause and manner of death. The time and place of death shall also be determined to the extent possible. Detailed color photographs of the deceased shall be included in the autopsy report in order to document and support the findings of the investigation. The autopsy report must describe any and all injuries to the deceased including any evidence of torture.

14. In order to ensure objective results, those conducting the autopsy must be able to function impartially and independently of any potentially implicated persons or organizations or entities.

15. Complainants, witnesses, those conducting the investigation and their families shall be protected from violence, threats of violence or any other form of intimidation. Those potentially implicated in extra-legal, arbitrary or summary executions shall be removed from any position of control or power, whether direct or indirect. over complainants, witnesses and their families, as well as over those conducting investigations.

16. Families of the deceased and their legal representatives shall be informed of, and have access to. any hearing as well as to all information relevant to the investigation, and shall be entitled to present other evidence. The family of the deceased shall have the right to insist that a medical or other qualified representative be present at the autopsy. When the identity of a deceased person has been determined, a notification of death shall be posted, and the family or relatives

of the deceased shall be informed immediately. The body of the deceased shall be returned to them upon completion of the investigation.

17. A written report shall be made within a reasonable period of time on the methods and findings of such investigations. The report shall be made public immediately and shall include the scope of the inquiry, procedures and methods used to evaluate evidence as well as conclusions and recommendations based on findings of fact and on applicable law. The report shall also describe in detail specific events that were found to have occurred and the evidence upon which such findings were based, and list the names of witnesses who testified, with the exception of those whose identities have been withheld for their own protection. The Government shall, within a reasonable period of time, either reply to the report of the investigation, or indicate the steps to be taken in response to it.

Legal proceedings

18. Governments shall ensure that persons identified by the investigation as having participated in extra-legal, arbitrary or summary executions in any territory under their jurisdiction are brought to justice. Governments shall either bring such persons to justice or cooperate to extradite any such persons to other countries wishing to exercise jurisdiction. This principle shall apply irrespective of who and where the perpetrators or the victims are, their nationalities or where the offence was committed.

19. Without prejudice to principle 3 above, an order from a superior officer or a public authority may not be invoked as a justification for extralegal, arbitrary or summary executions. Superiors, officers or other public officials may be held responsible for acts committed by officials under their authority if they had a reasonable opportunity to prevent such acts. In no circumstances, including a state of war, siege or other public emergency, shall blanket immunity from prosecution be granted to any person allegedly involved in extra-legal, arbitrary or summary executions.

20. The families and dependents of victims of extra-legal, arbitrary or summary executions shall be entitled to fair and adequate compensation within a reasonable period of time.